Empowerir
for the Highly Sensitive

"A fascinating exploration of our connection with the universe, backed by a strategic set of practical exercises to help us find our place in it—our balance, fulfillment, and joy. The author's friendly tone engages readers in a dialogue with themselves and helps them find the answers to all unspoken questions with ease."

~ **DIMITAR RIKOV,** editor in chief at
SoftPress Publishing, Bulgaria

"This book is true medicine for sensitive souls. Such guiding text was desperately needed and is also proof that God sends the right teachings at the right time. Bertold Keinar gives us simple yet profound tools to reach paradise on Earth and help us save ourselves and our species."

~ **THEODORA IOSSIFOVA,** founder and owner of Epica Center
for New Medicine, Bulgaria, and founder and president
of the Jerusalem Testament Foundation

"Being highly sensitive is normally viewed as a burden. This book insists that it can also be turned into a blessing. Furthermore, it supplies us with a toolbox—a set of exercises—for achieving this. If you are sensitive (and who isn't?), then this book is for you."

~ **NOAM URBACH,** owner of Shoket Contemporary Art, Israel

Empowering
Practices
for the
Highly Sensitive

An Experiential Guide
to Working with
Subtle Energies

Bertold Keinar

FINDHORN PRESS

Findhorn Press
One Park Street
Rochester, Vermont 05767
www.findhornpress.com

Text stock is SFI certified

Findhorn Press is a division of Inner Traditions International

Disclaimer
The information in this book is given in good faith and intended for
information only. Neither author nor publisher can be held liable by any
person for any loss or damage whatsoever which may arise from the use of this
book or any of the information therein.

Cataloging-in-Publication data for this title is available from the Library of Congress

ISBN 978-1-64411-492-6 (print)
ISBN 978-1-64411-493-3 (ebook)

Printed and bound in the United States by Lake Book Manufacturing Inc.
The text stock is SFI certified. The Sustainable Forestry Initiative® program
promotes sustainable forest management.

10 9 8 7 6 5 4 3 2 1

Edited by Jacqui Lewis
Text design and layout by Anna-Kristina Larsson
This book was typeset in Garamond, Spartan MB and Gabriela

To send correspondence to the author of this book, mail a first-class letter
to the author c/o Inner Traditions • Bear & Company, One Park Street,
Rochester, VT 05767, USA and we will forward the communication,
or contact the author directly at **bertoldkeinar@gmail.com**.

Contents

Introduction

There are many Highly Sensitive People (HSP) nowadays, walking around on our planet. Many of us were granted the permission to reincarnate during these times, times of transformation of Planet Earth. We, who decided to come here now, are thus developed souls—sensitive. Not all developed souls are sensitive, but those who have received this tool have been entrusted with it. We would be comfortable living in a balanced society, but Western society makes us suffer. By "Western society" I do not mean actually where you live but how you live (your rhythms and habits; you could live in Tibet or Nepal and live a "Western" life).

Many books have been written about spiritual development, practices and theory, but most of them, although they cover many topics of healthy lifestyle, energetic practices and meditation, don't directly address the problems (and where there is a problem there is an opportunity) facing sensitives in daily life. Very few books explain the logic and the structure of—the reason for—sensitivity, let alone the benefits of it from a spiritual perspective.

To be honest, I have never come across a book dealing with the topic of sensitives that is written from the perspective of a balanced person. Most of them seem to be written by people whose perception and thinking is dominated by the left side of the brain, and is thus imbalanced. The imbalance, the dominance of the left side of the brain in our lives, is the fundamental cause of suffering for sensitives. People like me who are authors and teachers and would like to help others can only help someone reach their own level, not beyond.

Sensitivity is a complex situation that needs a complex approach. Well, complex in the sense of how many aspects of life it affects. But in another way, everything is simple.

Our reality is multidimensional and we are multidimensional creatures. But we try to solve problems from the perspective of linear thinking—in other words, only from the left hemisphere of the brain. This means that we are trying to solve problems within the boundaries and with the way of thinking that created them. Our society does not look to solve problems but to eliminate the symptoms so as to make the subject comfortable for society and productive for the economy.

One example is the way we see and deal with emotions, mind, consciousness and subconsciousness. We see them as physiological phenomena and try to "train" them in the same way. We don't give them proper learning or attitude or try to balance them. We do not understand them at all, so how can we balance them?

Hypersensitivity, sensitivity and empathy do affect the physical body very much; however, as they come from our energetic bodies rather than the physical, they have to be addressed from this perspective. Sensitivity is a talent or a tool that our soul takes before incarnating, but this tool is so strong that we see it as a part of a person's nature or character. It cannot be taken away but it can be adjusted and controlled. The purpose of the tool we call sensitivity is to take in big amounts of information on a subtle level. It is a gift if we know how to use it, but a painful curse when we don't.

In this book you will find the reasons and explanations for your sensitivity, and the practical solutions to turn it from a burden to a blessing. The simple truth is: the bigger the potential for suffering, the bigger the potential for flourishing and happiness.

The Western reader is accustomed to receiving a lot of information and explanations from books (this is a logical and left-side-of-the-brain approach). We believe that if we read about transformation then we will experience it. But too much information without practice is actually doing more harm than good. The left side of the brain—in fact, the whole brain—is just one of the ways we receive and analyze information. For sensitive people, overengagement of the brain, particularly its left side, brings a lot of stress, discomfort and suffering.

The book includes information, explanations and practices. One of the purposes of the book is to switch your attention from the left side of the brain into balanced, whole-brain activity and to the other senses. The exercises are aimed at helping you to develop and balance what you already have and are designed to reflect your subtle structure. You must learn to do things from the perspectives you have, your sensitivity and beyond, step by step reducing the dominance of the left side of the brain.

I have written this book very much from my perspective: the perspective of a sensitive person, balanced and with strong intuition. A while ago, I was also living this suffering and imbalance, trying to fit into society and imitate its behavior.

The book contains all the information I think and hope might benefit you. I have largely assumed that I am writing for a reader who is on or is about to start on a spiritual path; but the exercises are for everyone—anyone can incorporate them into their life. So, if you don't like or agree with some parts, if things do not connect or resonate with you, or even if you find some of my words absurd, feel free to skip those parts—as long as you do keep in some way doing the exercises. Remember, we reach understanding and knowledge through experience, not theory. This book's exercises are experiences and they will teach you about their nature and your nature. You may not like all of the exercises or feel that they're compatible with you or yield much in the way of results, but I would still advise that you do all of them. The first reason to do the exercises is for the effect it has on us; but the experience we gain from doing them is also valuable and important. I would like you to try to find a way to keep at and succeed in those exercises that generate relatively lesser results. This is all part of self-learning.

The book is structured in a way that reflects a person's inner balance, rather than being a purely left-side-of-the-brain creation. It contains a lot of heart, goodwill and love. Read from the heart, understand it with intuition and give it time.

Anything you don't understand, leave for later. I deliberately mention many things without explanation, as they are elaborated on at their proper place in the book. Just keep reading and follow the instructions and you will find what you are looking for.

Note: Throughout the book the word "heart" will appear many times, sometimes as an idea of the expression of the soul, sometimes as a reference to the energetic equivalent of the heart and sometimes to the physical organ.

This book will help you to learn, among other things: a general idea of how some of the subtle bodies work, and their structure; how to adjust your sensitivity; how to protect yourself; how to open and balance some of the chakras; how to operate in the "alpha realm"; how to connect to your godly source, how to meditate, how to balance the immediate aspects of your existence (to which your awareness has already reached); the logic behind (some) esoteric practices; about your subconscious and how to communicate with it; cleansing fears (and other rubbish you do not need); controlling energies; karma; inner peace, self-esteem, love, happiness, emotions and energies; how to trust your senses rather than logic—and (of course) more . . .

I wish you pleasant reading and a fruitful journey.

1

Who Are the Sensitives?

Highly sensitive people don't really need anyone to tell them "who sensitive people are." They don't need any definitions from third parties (I say "they"; I mean "we"). We just know we feel too much from our surroundings, from the people around us, from the emotions of others, from the present and the past . . . and we cannot put all this information in order. It leaves its imprints on us, sometimes for a long time; and too many imprints cloud our nature. They are like impressions, we tend to act upon them.

Sensitives feel too much, both within ourselves and from outside. We are empaths. Strange ability—it seems to have no use in Western society. But in fact it does have a use for us; it is a very important tool. I believe too that intuition and sensitivity is the future and will one day be a requirement for some professions.

The only way to figure out why this tool is so important for you is to learn from living with it. Live with it when it is balanced and when you are in balance, and it is serving your path and the people around you. After you learn to use it, you will not think that "too much feeling" exists. So it is important to first learn about it and how to balance it.

In Western society, people live in the left side of their brain. The left side is about analyzing, calculating, dismantling and assembling. It is linear and limited. The symptoms when we are unbalanced and life is too much focused on this include feeling overwhelmed by negative emotions, getting obsessive over things and going unnecessarily deep into things.

Who do we consider smart in our society? Physicists, doctors, mathematicians, lawyers, engineers, software developers—in short, left-hemisphere thinkers. Most of the existing programs for brain and IQ development are aimed at the left side of the brain.

Who is running our society? Conducting research and writing academic papers? Telling us from the TV screen that they have carried out new research that proves this and that? They tell us what we need to be afraid of and why. The "why" is very important. The why makes people with rational thinking (and rational only) "buy" whatever they are being sold from the TV screen. We are ruled by people whose brains are misbalanced. That is how they see the world and that is how they rule us. This is how our society, government and architecture (most of our buildings are square and without round elements) are built. This is how we process and understand the world. This is also how we "teach" our kids to live.

School, especially in the past although things are changing, has been mainly about the left side of the brain, about dismantling notions and putting them together—the process of understanding with the left brain.

Imbalanced people can be easily ruled and manipulated. They accept everything that sounds plausible, rational or logical (logical, as opposed to truthful, means able to sustain an argument with inner integrity). Imbalanced people are easily influenced by their negative emotions (negative in this context means survival-related emotions, associated with the lower three chakras). This is because the left side of the brain has to deliver a solution, to be one of the components of the whole, not be treated as the whole. It is driven by emotions, normally negative ones because negative emotions are a problem and the brain looks for solutions. It tends to overdo its job of looking for a solution and so its original motivation (the negative emotion that triggered the brain operation) becomes chronic. The brain will keep looking for a better solution due to the fact that the negative emotion that triggered the operation has never left. Instead, this negative emotion becomes second nature.

The left side of the brain acts like a washing machine that washes the same clothes over and over again. Chronically solving existential problems (survival mode), rethinking the same piece of data, the brain's left side makes us constantly believe that we are in survival mode, and so our energetic resources cannot be directed to inner happiness, let alone spiritual growth. From the moment our energies are caught by the left side of the brain using negative emotions as fuel, the energy from the lower chakras cannot rise above the third chakra. This stage is harmful to anyone, let alone sensitive people. If you are seeking spiritual development, you will not be able to reach it unless you solve this problem.

Living the "left-sided" life as a sensitive person makes this situation even worse. It goes against the nature of the balance in which sensitives have to stay, and their sensitivity towards other people's feelings and emotions makes them an easy "target." It is hard work having to deal not just with your own survival emotions (blown out of proportions by the left side of the brain) but also with all the other people close to you. Just think briefly of someone you know—someone in your family, a child, a sexual partner, a friend; someone who lives with you, or someone you see every day at work. Did you feel it? the feeling that came up in you while reading the last few lines? With people who have caused you some sort of trauma, even on a small scale, when you think of them, the memory comes into your consciousness as a reflection of the trauma.

Sensitive people "recollect" the feeling of others' energies; so they recollect the feeling of a person with not-pleasant energies just by thinking of them. These people become an association to the trauma or negative event. This is the negative side of being an—imbalanced—sensitive person.

The tricky part is that from the moment you get the negative emotions there is no coming back. You either wait long enough for it to sink in, or make a huge effort to convince yourself that there is nothing to be afraid of or worry about. Negative emotion is very hard to get rid of (I say *emotion* for the sake of simplicity; it includes thoughts as well).

But the good news for you is that that is possible; and actually very easy, if you know how.

Negative emotions are very contagious, especially when you are sensitive—then you are extra-vulnerable. After being exposed to the world of negative emotions and thoughts of the people who are close to you whether by choice or by fate, you get overloaded and close yourself off, run away or look for a place where you can feel safe. Normally, those are the places where your sensitivity is not sensitive any more. When we don't have people around us, we have less to sense. When we are alone we are calmer, because we have no one to sense. Our sensitivity is also less receptive in other states, like after drinking alcohol or taking drugs. These temporarily "switch off" sensitivity, although not other things like energetic imprints and unprotected alpha state (about which we will talk later).

Those states of sedation aren't solving the problem. The means of sedation does not protect you from the outer world's energies and emotions. All they do, at best, is to put you in a non-sensitive mode. You stop feeling but the processes keep running. The even more harmful aspect of sedation means (like marijuana) is that they produce a deeper stage of meditative trance mode. This mode is a very vulnerable one for sensitives and for those who meditate. At this stage the brain is in the alpha wave state; at this stage we are more receptive and open to other kinds of information and (to some extent) to our subconscious. Sensitive people are already, most of the time, at least some way into the alpha state and very receptive to it. This is the reason why we feel so intensely the range of feelings and energies around us.

If we use the means of sedation in an unprotected way, a thick layer of "dark" energies covers all our senses (including a big part of our awareness), to prevent us from feeling the outer world and all its individuals. This thick layer comes between your etheric body and the other bodies, eventually reducing your sensitivity. But the energy flow is also reduced. From that moment on, your energy cannot reach your bodies, and this will cause illnesses in the future.

Childhood can be a time of grace for some of us sensitives, but when puberty hits, we lose the inner connection with ourselves and the world turns its back on us. It happens to everyone. When we become teenagers, we wake up to a new reality and begin to look for ourselves, because of inner disconnection. Some sensitive people start to look inside for the connection they had before, but in vain. Later we usually try to find the answers outside. But the farther we go, the fewer answers we get. Some of us never find the answers.

The universe serves one purpose: spiritual growth. Our planet is the school for mastering (among other things) the emotions and thoughts in the physical body. There are three kinds of people on our planet from the point of view of what their motivation is; those who run away from pain (pain is BAD) those who chase pleasure (pleasure is GOOD), and those who seek the truth or spiritual growth (there is not good or bad; everything is there to serve the purpose of spiritual evolution, personally and collectively). Apart from the last type (truth-seekers) we have three main episodes in life: childhood, karma and post-karma (it is very individual and varies between people, but I like to see it and express it that way for simplicity). The first two types can stay in the stage of karma all their lives, paying and accumulating karma. Even when they have finished the karma period they do not always manage to re-establish themselves and cleanse away the effects of this period.

2

How to Read This Book

If you are ready for the truths (principles) described in the book you will accept them, you will understand them with the heart and with your intuition. You will be able to put those truths into practice. It is no use accepting truths like dogmas. In dogmas there is no understanding and no growth, and maybe no truths. If you cannot relate to some of what is in this book, just skip them for now. Some of the truths will be accepted now, others will be seeded for future understanding.

I don't ask you to follow the book blindly, but do try not to distance yourself from things that bring inconvenience. Try the exercises and examine and explore everything for yourself. Feel the energy of each exercise flowing through you before accepting things completely. Even then, question whether you did and felt it the right way. Be patient and positive. If you are ready and holding this book, it means you are somewhere on the way to inner peace and balance.

In spiritual development truths are more accurately thought of as "principles." The things you practice now are the things that are your ceiling, thus the truth. After being introduced to higher principles you will understand that your truths are only half-truths. Absolute truths become relative and at this point we are introduced to new absolute truths. Absolute truths are temporary.

Spiritual development is raising the level of your truths.

Spiritual development is raising your consciousness to the level of new truth. When we speak about truth we imagine something absolute; but the only thing that is absolute is God. Our consciousness is on the journey to the "center" of God. This journey is eternal, thus it never meets absolute truth. As long as our consciousness is not introduced to a higher principle the current principle is the absolute truth.

This is very visible in kids; for them every day is a discovery of a new principle. Among adults only a few keep discovering higher principles, normally in scientific investigations.

All goals become means for higher goals. This is the normal path of all development. Something intrigues me today and I want to learn and master it. When I have it as a part of me, the next thing, which is related to the first, catches my attention, and I set myself to reach it. The new thing has opened only thanks to my previous achievements.

As a sensitive person I wanted protection, after getting protection I wanted balance, then spiritual development, and I understood that my soul, me as the higher aspects, which take the place of the everyday personality, wants to serve. Then I look for ways to serve other people, and every service becomes a step to a higher service. Of course service has to come within the boundaries of one's personal path too.

Note: Speaking of God is a very sensitive and complicated topic. Our life is researching what God is, by all the means we have: physical, mental, emotional; calmness, silences, higher aspects of Love and so on. When I say "God" here I mean the source of all, the beginning of all, the preliminary Ideal that carries in it all other ideas. If we try to track any notion to where it begins, eventually we will reach our idea of God.

Every unit in this book begins with a small title and ends with one main exercise and a few complementary ones. I would kindly ask you to leave some time between each unit. This time is necessary for processing and integration of new vibrations and habits developed by the exercises. The real transformation is in the exercises, not in the theory.

The main exercise is a must, the complementary ones are very strongly recommended. The main and the complementary exercises, in most cases, are directed at solving one and the same "technical" issue. Once you feel comfortable with the main exercise, you can try some or all of the complementary ones. Once you feel that you are in control and are hungry for more, proceed to the next unit.

The book is built in such a way that every exercise builds the "muscle" for the next one. If you go step by step, you will have all the tools to succeed in the next exercise and develop understanding of inner things (this why you have sensitivity, among other reasons—to be able to sense the inner).

In many cases I keep the explanations for later. It is the same with the exercises. If I do not specify a timeframe, it is because I am leaving you to find the right one. Since this book aims to put you in balance, there are many things regarding the exercises that I leave you to figure out. Try to feel, fail, keep practicing and get better. In other words, grow. And when you are totally on it, let it go and proceed to the next . . .

Three Periods of Life

Childhood: during this period we receive all the seeds we need to deal with the karma and post-karma periods. We are engaged with all kinds of activities that will be opened up in the future. Meaning, we touch and experience many things. We try to do things we like (we call it playing). We sow the seeds through joy. Joy is the sign that signals to us that what we are doing comes from the root of our soul and has something to do with our future on Earth.

Why do we like some games more than others? Why do some things we do or learn come hand in hand with pleasure or joy? Kids like to have fun. Joy comes when we touch things that are special for us, that have connection with our self-fulfillment on Earth. Joy is connected to our path on Earth; it comes to us from higher dimensions.

Remember the inner connection to ourselves, the one that gets lost during puberty? While we are kids it is very strong within us. This is the connection between God (our godly spark), the big spirit, and the spark within us. Water runs in pipes and electricity in cables; joy runs in this inner connection. All the positive emotions do, but this one is especially important in our life, and as an indicator for our direction in the post-karma period. Later we are going to connect to all the points of joy we had during childhood. All the seeds we sowed in the childhood period.

The more experiences and memories we have from this time the easier it is going to be for us later. In the post-karma period, those small memories will pop up unpredictably, pointing to us and hinting, pointing to the things we liked to do, the things that brought us joy as kids. Those moments are there to show us our direction.

During this period another process is happening too: the process of imprinting past and future lessons. We come with a certain karma, some energies from the past, some lessons we have not finished and some doubts we have towards the universe. When we are born, we don't remember those unfinished matters but we carry the energies of them within us (some of them can be seen on the natal chart). Those energies will manifest an event in our childhood, which later we will address as trauma. Those lessons to be learned will be resolved during the karma period. In other words, our traumatic childhood experiences are the result of karmic debts and lessons. I am saying this because we tend to blame the "event" or other people for our misfortunes and traumas that stay with us all our lives; but in reality, we are responsible for the appearance of these events in our lives—we attracted them.

Childhood is our preparation time. It lets us unfold and develop some of the things we have to reach eventually. In childhood, we are shown what is expected from us from the point of view of doing and reaching. In childhood we are, if not at the peak, above the midpoint of our conditionally fulfilled potential. "Conditionally" because it is shown to us and then taken away from us, so we can achieve it by our own means.

For those of us who have accumulated karma, reincarnation is inevitable. In this way, karma and incarnations are inseparable. Reincarnation is the expression of and opportunity for the accumulated karma to be learned and cleaned. We see someone who has talent in a certain sphere and we think "this person is gifted." But in fact, this person was working hard to develop this "gift" in their previous lives. We think, this kid is nothing like his parents, why? Because parents don't give characters to kids, only channel some talents. Children are souls with their own "character" and their own experience that has been accumulated in previous incarnations. Most of us carry "luggage" from previous incarnations, and this is karma. It is a combination of paybacks (good and bad), lessons and tests.

Our society likes to see us all as a *tabula rasa*. When we come to this world, the thinking is, we have only two main sources of influence on our development: environment and genetics. In fact, we come here with pretty much fixed preferences and tastes. We have what makes us happy and what we have to pay for. The rest is how this previous experience interacts with our environment and genetics.

So, during puberty, after a certain period of transformation during which, normally, the process of inner disconnection takes place, we are left with the lessons, tests and doubts we have to face in this life.

At the beginning of this period, some of us are still thinking and acting using the "old," childhood way of thinking and dealing with the world (as if we are still connected to the source). This inner connection gives security and intuition. It is there to illustrate what we have to accomplish in the future. Then comes the disconnection that leaves us with what we have to do. It is like a sports coach: they give you a speech before you step on the field, but from then on, you are by yourself.

The loss of the inner connection is what exposes our vulnerability and lack of self-esteem. The things that are on the negative side of sensitivity. The connection was the thing that was protecting us. This connection maintained the "supply line" from the higher part of ourselves, the part that was protecting us. From the moment it ceases to operate we lose not just the protection but also our identity. Our higher identity switches to a lower, "you are on your own," sort of identity.

The karma period is the period of our life in which we are disconnected from our higher part and are operating as our lower self, the character. We are about to learn our lessons while being partially blind (otherwise it wouldn't be so significant for our soul). It is our dark ages before the Renaissance, if you like.

Many of us, normally during our teenage years, cultivate a new "cool" identity. After facing the emptiness caused by the disconnection, we begin looking around, out, for what to fill this hole with. We find or develop a new identity that we identify ourselves with. This identity has nothing to do with our (real) selves but we are afraid to lose it because we are afraid of the emptiness, of the disconnection we experienced after our inner connection broke.

This period is different for everyone. In many cases it reaches its apotheosis in some very hard lessons. These lessons can come in the form of sickness, divorce, painful work loss or other life-changing events. For some people, the painful events mark the beginning and the end of the period. During the "apotheosis" time and later, it is very important not to hold on to the past, to what is leaving. It is important to accept the changes in a healthy way.

Many moments of light will come during this time. People find themselves doing things they have not done for a very long time. Those things are, in many cases, the same as the ones we liked to do during childhood. We return to them to recharge, because during these moments we feel alive; those moments give us life.

As a matter of fact, the karma period can be easier if we understand that we have lost the connection and if we know how to regain it. Not many of us are born into a family of yogis or spiritual and esoteric teachers. But if we keep reading this book, we will understand how to do it. No path on this planet is easy, but setting off on the path consciously, with the proper knowledge and tools, will be easier; there will be fewer punches to the head and more understanding of the process.

Post-karma: After the karmic peak is over, normally between the ages of thirty-five and forty-five (although for some people it is much later), and the emotional turmoil is quietening (for some it might be mental turmoil instead, or both), comes the post-karmic period. The midlife crisis we all know about can be in many cases related to the beginning of this stage, the post-apotheosis stage of the karma period from above. While living or fighting the lessons of the karma period of our life, we develop tools, ways of thinking and perception of environment that surrounds us. We have forgotten that we were kids, we have forgotten that we were teenagers. We only remember ourselves from the moment of us being able to manage to put our lives together after each event of disconnection and hard lessons.

The emptiness that comes in the post-karma period scares some of us. We try to rethink our lives and find our path. For some, nothing has really changed: no hard lessons, no tremendous changes; but the emptiness is there. This emptiness is caused by the "cleansing" of the old energies from your life, making room for new ones. This "cleansing" can be very traumatic. Those events that turn our life upside down are due to this.

Some people cannot really manage this emptiness and try to fill it with meaning. Others try to go back to their old way of life. This is the time when you need to remember your moments of joy. This is the time when the universe tells you that your lesson is over, you are trained and ready to fulfill all your desires. Those actions that were bringing joy into your life are still potentially there, still the pipes in which run the energy, the joy, your creational energy.

The key here is very simple, although not many of us are aware of it. The principle says that you cannot reach the next peak of activity in your life using the tools with which you reached the previous peak. Peaks, apotheosis, emptiness are all part of the law of rhythm. See how it repeats itself.

In boxing and martial arts, for example, the teacher lets the more experienced students help less experienced students, sometimes even to teach them all the basics. This is exactly the same as our principle. How many times have you felt you were at the peak of something, but then after explaining it to someone else, this feeling of "I'm so confident about this material" has left you, leaving emptiness? But it also leaves the potential for future peaks. After the release of the old energy, the energy of the old peak, we can then receive future successes.

In the post-karma period or our midlife crisis, we are at the beginning of our new life. We have the emptiness, so where shall we look for the next peak of our lives? The clues are in the past. All the moments of joy we had in our childhood will come back to us if we allow; the things we love are available to us. Now is the time to connect to points of joy from our childhood and elevate them, just as the great minds of the Renaissance and the scientific revolution of the Enlightenment were able to do great things with the knowledge they received from the classic age. History follows the same principle.

We have already looked at the brain's alpha waves and something about how this state is an unprotected state and how exactly it makes us sensitive. People have different levels of consciousness. Let us concentrate on the next three: subconsciousness, consciousness and super-consciousness.

Super-consciousness is the one we are trying to reach, the one we are eager to achieve from the moment we understand that this life has more to offer. This is the realm to which the truth-seekers are traveling.

Consciousness is the one we are present in during our waking hours. It is our daily life (except for some moments during the day). It is, more or less, being present in what is happening around us. It is much more complicated, but this simple way of illustration has one purpose: to bring us to the subconsciousness.

The subconsciousness lies in the realm of our dreams. This is a subtle level of our esoteric structure to which we believe we don't have conscious access. This area is constructed of the not-manifested energy, the quantum field of possibilities if you like. This is water, formless sea. And when something influences some part of this sea to form a shape, this shape influences and projects itself into our daily life. Some painful event is engraved into our subconsciousness through the influence of strong emotion.

It is very important to understand more of the nature of this vast sea we call subconsciousness because it lies in the realm of subtle energies, emotions, thoughts. This is the place where many creatures exist. Your access there is via the alpha state of the brain.

Alpha waves have levels or degrees; going into higher alpha state is actually going deeper, like with meditation. From this point of view, sensitive people are in the alpha-waves state most of the time, even if this state is not very deep. We are sensitive because, like in the film *The Matrix,* we are connected to this subtle reality and that is why we feel the subtle energetic communication more strongly. We are partially living in the world, at a certain level of existence, from which we receive constant feedback. This subtle world is full of life and some of this life can be harmful to us. It is like traveling to a new place; it is better if we are equipped to meet the uncertainty and the potential dangers. But that is exactly what we do: we go to the alpha state without protection.

When we are connected to the field of subtle communication of energies, and we see someone's negative emotions, they are being imprinted in our subtle reality, on our subtle bodies and in our subconsciousness.

It is even more than that. If our subconsciousness lies on a certain level of reality, subtler reality, what is the logical conclusion? That everyone's subconsciousness is located in the same place, on the same frequency of reality. The "collective unconscious" of Carl Jung, if you like. When we go into trance or meditation we reach the same realm, and in this realm we can find our subconsciousness.

It is important to mention that our consciousness is the interpreter of the events of our life. If we almost got hit by a car and took it easily and calmly (because the consciousness thinks we were lucky), there will be nothing negative imprinted in the subconsciousness. But if we are scared and panicked by the event, it will be written in the subconsciousness. Our consciousness makes the difference.

If we have a negative experience that comes along with strong emotion, this experience is going to enter our subconsciousness even more strongly. And if something can enter . . . ? Right, it can exit. So the subtle shared realm where our subconsciousness lies is the key to our sensitivity.

Reading this book is a process of transformation, a gradual one. The process contains two sides: transformation of the way we think (all this information in the book) and the way we live (all the exercises and new habits). So now is a good time to introduce the first exercise.

main exercise

The (morning) candle

Time and duration

First thing in the morning for 5 minutes.

What to do

Take a simple candle, light it and put it in front of you (a hand to a hand-and-a-half away) and visualize it.

How to do it

Take a few moments to memorize the candle. After you are sure you have an image of it, close your eyes and visualize the candle in the center of your head (don't worry too much about locating the physical center). If you wish to be more accurate, visualize it at the pineal gland (again, don't worry too much about physical accuracy). When you have it there, look at it, let your concentration be on it. Stay on the image of the candle you have created in your mind for the whole period of 5 minutes. There has to be only silence and candle.

As you do it more, you should work on making the image of the candle more elaborate. Begin to see more details of the candle in the image you create in your mind. Details like texture, color, contours, and reflections.

What not to do

- Don't fight or suppress your thoughts. Thoughts will come. Just keep concentrating on the candle. If you catch yourself daydreaming and led away by your stream of thoughts, just come back to the candle.
- Don't introduce distractions by combining it with other things—music, TV, meals or anything else.

- Don't do the exercise for more than 5 minutes, even if you only concentrated on the candle for 10 seconds and for the rest you were flying in the skies.
- If a feeling appears, don't switch your concentration to the feeling (even if it is a very pleasant one); stay on the image of the candle.

How and when do I know it's working?

People who meditate or do other related practices will usually feel the effect kick-in within three to five days.

For other people it will take a bit longer. I cannot really say how long. But just keep doing the exercise. If you don't feel the effect, maybe you have put the image in the wrong place in your head, or you aren't concentrating on the candle. Play with it till you find the right place. And keep working on concentrating on it. You train yourself by persistence and repetition.

It may sound like it will take months, but it won't; it is a relatively easy and fast-working exercise.

Why am I doing it?

Sensitive people are sensitive because they feel energies, so they have to deal somehow with these energies. This exercise strengthens the concentration and awakens the organ that, together with the concentration, will control those energies. The power of concentration is the power of will, and the energies follow the will.

So very simple

Morning, candle, 5 minutes only, no distractions.

This is the most basic but the most important exercise. If you don't want to do it, there is really no point in going any further; you should close this book now. Seriously, this exercise is very fundamental and important and reading further without taking it on would be a waste of time.

At this stage it is a good idea to put the book aside for a week, or, alternatively, reread what you've read until this point. But don't read any further at the moment. Do the candle exercise for seven days. Otherwise the main exercise in the next section (the energetic balls exercise) will not work.

Remember we looked at how our Western society develops only one side of the brain? And how it gets in the way of us finding balance? Here are some more examples.

We have two hands and two eyes. Most of us use one hand as a dominant hand; and the same for the eyes. What hand are you holding the book with? You probably always hold books with the same hand, your dominant one. Our imbalance is part of our habits.

What is the solution? Start engaging your other, non-dominant hand in your daily life; gradually give it more "responsibilities." Use it for brushing your teeth, washing the dishes, opening doors and so on. Keep redirecting more actions to the non-dominant hand until all is left for the original dominant one is handling knives, and writing. When you feel confident enough, start using the hand for cutting bread and vegetables. But do it slowly!

It is interesting to observe, when you switch hands, how you will still try to apply your old thinking approach. But with time, you will see how the "new" hand uses other patterns of thinking and doing things rather than always taking the linear, step-by-step option. It is fun. You will like it.

As for the eyes, what do we know from school? We learned that two eyes are needed to see in dimensions, to see depth. But what do we look at all day? Screens, tablets, "smart" phones, TVs, books, written material like books and whatnot, but all are FLAT. What happens when we look at flat objects all day? We develop a "dominant" eye and a "lazy" eye. And it is not just the flat objects that we look at all day, it is also the constant concentration of the eye; we concentrate on dots, small symbols. Where is the other side? The unfocused vision? The eyes, actually, are more important for balance than the hands. Hands balance the two hemispheres of the brain, eyes activate the pineal gland, which is responsible for the whole balance of the bodies and energies. When your eyes are not used properly (God gave you two eyes for a reason, not for having one dominant and one lazy) your pineal gland stops fulfilling most of its balancing operations.

In yoga, for instance, when we do *asanas* (postures) we balance the previous *asana* with a compensating or complementary one. Our inhales and exhales are equal—breathing is rhythmic and balanced. We are calm and relaxed but the flow of the energy through our four lower bodies is strong again, balanced.

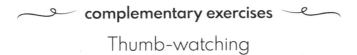

complementary exercises
Thumb-watching

Time and duration

Do it as much as you can; it is a short exercise, only needing 2-3 minutes (or longer, if you wish). But don't overload the eyes; do it gently and gradually. Do it before bed.

What to do

Look at your thumbnails, the left eye looking at the left nail and the right eye at the right. You can put something attractive on the nail to make it easier for the eye to lock onto the nail—red erasable marker, a small sticker—whatever you like, you get the point.

How to do it

Make a fist, leaving your thumbs up; now put them next to each other so the thumbnails face you. Bring them close enough to the face so you can effortlessly look at each nail with the corresponding eye (left at left, right at right).

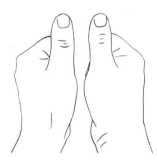

After a while, when you feel ready, start moving the hands away from the face, slowly. Keep the eyes on the nails in the same way. Move the hands away from the face, holding each eye on its spot and focused. When you lose focus or one of the eyes "decides" to quit the exercise, stop, pull the hands back to the last position at which both eyes looked at their corresponding nail, and start moving the hands away and back towards the face with small movements (back and forth, as if you're trying to push the limit of the eyes to stay focused on the nails more).

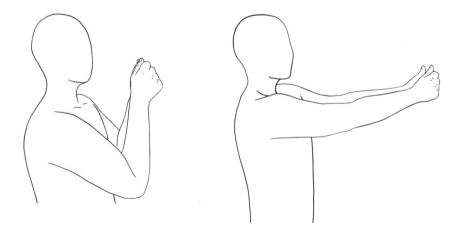

When you feel overloaded or tired, stop the exercise. Return to it after a while or the next day. It is important not to drop the hands but to bring them back together and pull them closer to the face to the position at which the eyes feel relaxed, or even the original position.

Keep moving your hands away (while keeping the eyes on their spots) more and more every time you practice. As you advance, you will eventually move your hands and stretch your arms out to their maximum stretch. Once you've reached this point, start opening the hands out, by moving them in different directions away from each other. Keep each eye on its nail, using the same principle as before: reach the maximum, then go back a bit and make small movements out and in. After finishing, don't forget to bring the hands to a comfortable position for the eyes and then end the exercise.

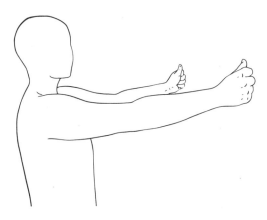

When you move the hands away from each other, a weird field appears. You know when you look at the road on a hot day, you see a moving layer of air? This is very similar to the field that appears between the thumbs.

This field is very important, because when your pineal gland wakes up, it concentrates on this field. Remember this, it is essential. Only as the two eyes get balanced can the third eye wake up. (The third eye and the pineal gland are not the same but are related; I would say cousins.)

What not to do

- Don't overdo it; don't overload the eyes. If you feel tired, stop.
- Try to have a simple and blank background. Don't have anything there that can attract the eyes.
- Don't play with focus. Just move the hands slowly back and forth, away and towards each other. Slowly.

How and when do I know it's working?

Looking at flat objects imbalances our eyes. One becomes lazy and the other dominant. With time, you will get back to seeing everything in 3D. You will notice that both eyes do their fair share of *seeing*. Another sign that you are advancing with the exercise is the field that appears between the thumbs. This indicates that the pineal gland is becoming activated, which is a sign of balance.

Why am I doing it?

You are balancing and evenly redistributing the load on your eyes. Gradually, hopefully, you will start using both eyes equally. At some point—very soon if you combine it with other exercises—your pineal gland will wake up. The pineal gland is also a kind of eye and it has a bigger range of sight than both eyes combined.

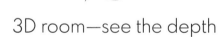

3D room—see the depth

Time and duration

A few times a day for a few seconds.

What to do

To see the room in 3D, to see the depth of the room.

How to do it

Try to see the distance between you and the furthest corner of the room as a field that has volume, like it is full of water and you are trying to look at the water and the shape it takes to fill the space. Now see the whole volume and the shape as one piece, feel it, then release. With time you will be able to see the room in 3D. When that happens, stop doing the exercise. With time, you will be able easily and for a long time, to concentrate on the field in the room or in any other place.

What not to do

As in the previous exercise (as you can see, they are very similar), don't overload the eyes. As in sport, overdoing it harms the muscles instead of strengthening them.

How and when do I know it's working?

You will start using both eyes and seeing the depth of space and the field. When you see the 3D, both eyes work; when you see the field the pineal gland wakes up.

Why am I doing it?

This series of exercises has one goal: to balance the eyes and activate the pineal gland. This is the beginning of balance.

In short

See the depth, see the field, see 3D; find balance.

Candle flame aura

Time and duration

Morning or evening, after work or before bed. For a few minutes, but again, don't overload the eyes.

What to do
See the aura of the flame of the candle.

How to do it
In a dim room, light a candle and try to see its aura. When you are able to see it, keep your attention on it. You will most probably try to play with your focus to "grasp" the aura by concentrating your vision on it; but if you do this it will disappear. The key here is to keep the eyes unfocused and still see the aura.

The pineal gland can see it clearly; when you direct the main responsibility of seeing to the pineal gland, you will see the aura clearly. The moment you engage the focus of the eyes, you will lose it.

What not to do
You already know . . .

How and when do I know it's working?
When you are able to easily switch from focused sight to defocused sight and see the field.

Why am I doing it?
The more balance we achieve the more hidden abilities are opened. By engaging the eye we use less; we can balance the work of the brain, which gives us access to the pineal gland, which means we can access the crown chakra.

In short
Make sure the room is dim; see the aura of the flame for a short time. Take care not to overload the eyes.

Defocusing the eyesight

Time and duration
Any time you want for any duration, as long as you don't overload the eyes.

What to do
Defocus the eyes and see the field.

How to do it
If you have been doing the above exercises you already have enough tools and experience to figure it out.

What not to do
I believe you already have a sense of what not to do. I'll just remind you not to overload the eyes.

How and when do I know it's working
Use your intuition.

Why am I doing it
You already know.

In short
Awaken the pineal gland, see the field and let the brain get into balance.

3

Some of the Subtle Bodies

The subject of the subtle bodies is vast, but the focus of this book is balancing, so I have kept the section on the subtle bodies short and have focused on only the relevant angle and information.

As well as having their own functions and qualities, subtle bodies influence each other. High vibrational bodies influence the lower ones. For example, with thoughts you can reason your emotions; and with emotions, you can create a healthy or unhealthy physical body. However, you cannot influence with your physical body the emotional or the mental. This does not mean that if you have pain your emotions and thoughts are not relevant; it just means that they cannot be changed permanently. With our physical body we react through emotions and thoughts, but we cannot design or shape our thoughts or emotions with our physical body.

So in many of the exercises in this book, and in life (like guided meditations and visualizations), we don't work with our physical body but with the subtle bodies. It takes time to develop sensitivity to each body and it might be tricky at the beginning for some people. But all we have to remember is not to work with the physical body, but with the subtle bodies, even if we can't distinguish between them.

Different schools describe different bodies based on the number of them or their functions. Most agree on the basics but with some variations. There are different energetic frequencies of existence (consciousness): like emotions, mental, and beyond. Some schools call all the levels bodies but in fact, only three levels have bodies: the physical, the emotional (astral) and the mental. The rest are more like planes of existence, levels of consciousness or dimensions.

Etheric Body

Subtle bodies are energetic fields (from the physical point of view). On this level, we can see how those fields begin in the spine and from there project themselves around the physical body. We call this projection around the body "the aura," and the energetic centers in the aura we know as "chakras." These energetic fields are in and around the body and they penetrate each other. The chakras are located at the etheric double or etheric body.

So why is it so important for us sensitives to know about those bodies and their structure? Actually, it is highly important. The most basic particle we can call "I am," regardless of its consciousness level (let's call it Spirit) is connected (or dressed) to those subtle bodies, the energetic fields. The whole functional side of the spirit sensing the physical environment is through the connection between "I am" and the energetic bodies.

But it is more than just sensing; it is the ability to experience and express emotion and turn your thoughts into energetic reality (create). The spirit belongs to a pure realm, the purest realm. The spirit has the ability to create, but even the best architect needs tools and matter to create. The tools of the spirit in our Earthly existence are those subtle bodies. The matter is all around us, endless volumes of it, and we know it by the name *prana*.

We can conclude that the two basic elements of creation (the manifestation of the Great mind, the Big Spirit) are Spirit and matter. Spirit is God's particle, which is simultaneously the Godlike particle. Everything else we can see as matter, from the heaviest matter that we call physical, to the subtlest matter. Somewhere between those two extremes on the matter scale are our subtle bodies and *prana* (in all its forms). Again, we are looking at things here from the perspective of what's relevant to us.

Note: Some see God as the updated version of themselves, which is in essence true. Think the ultimate version. We come from God and we have God's abilities as potential. Spiritual evolution is unfolding those abilities.

The first subtle body that dresses the "I am" is the Aether or Ether. Some people call it a "body," but it is more of an energetic field. This is the substance that, among other functions, makes it possible for us to feel the environment and the connection and the function of the other bodies. We can call it the feedback field. It helps the spirit to get feedback from "reality" and to deliver energy to everywhere it reaches. It is like if we had the internet in electrical sockets and received both information exchange and energy. In short, ether channels energy and information. Ether is actually rather more complicated than this, but we are going to keep things simple.

Since this substance is the conductor of energy, it has to be spread all over the physical body and to reach every cell of it. Our inner life (organism) and the health state depends on getting energy, vitality, *prana*. But this field is a conductor of information and feelings, remember? So when we feel pain, hunger or heavy energies around us we tend to shrink it or move it from the organs or areas where we sense pain.

Imagine you enter a room, and it is very hard for you to be in this room. The "atmosphere" is not nice, you think to yourself. There are undesirable energies in it. Those energies are incompatible with you. Maybe they are negative emotions or thoughts from the past that someone has left there (did I mention that ether records everything? I'll mention it now), or a simple lack of circulating *prana*. So you enter this room, and have to stay there. And you feel all kinds of weird, very unpleasant things. If you knew how to protect yourself, then you could, but you don't. Every time those weird feelings reach a peak, you "suck" your energetic field of ether in.

The same happens when you are standing queuing for hot dogs or lipstick. When you feel too much of your surroundings. When you are stuck on a twelve-hour flight near someone who is obviously a nervous flyer, or anyone who is in your zone of feeling (remember that this field extends out of the body, so you feel things going on around you regardless of if they touch you or not). It's the same with inner discomfort; like when you're hungry but don't eat because you are very busy or distracted by other things. Or if you have and ignore a toothache or menstrual pain, or you're wearing clothes or shoes that are uncomfortable, or ignore bad sexual experiences or trauma. We disregard the needs of the body like this on a regular basis.

The fundamental side of many (if not all) illnesses, regardless of their cause, is lack of ether. Over time, we exhaust our energetic resources. Things including stress, lack of proper food or good eating habits, bad air quality, poor breathing habits and any kind of uncomfortable clothing, all make you suck in your ether body to stop feeling. Sensitivity, then, can be a cause of illnesses. But it can also be the tool to cure yourself, and help all those around you. You can be—or already are—a healer.

When we have difficulty thinking, the brain is slow, we suck energy from all parts of the body below the head and in many cases we include the ether. Why do old people not have strength in their hands? Why do martial arts practitioners have strong hands? When you are trying to open a jar of jam or pickles, you bring energy and ether to the hands. Martial art practitioners train their hands so they have a lot of ether in them. And some old people, unfortunately, suck ether from the hands and the body to the head and the eyes. Sprinters have most of their ether in the legs, boxers in the arms and upper chest. When we focus on the taste of food we move the ether to the mouth.

Ether is important, then, and you have to keep it in the body and keep it well distributed around the body. Practicing yoga, qigong and tai ji quan (tai chi) in the proper way redistributes and recharges the ether throughout the body. By getting into proper and steady balance we can solve this problem for good and learn to cure ourselves—or let the energy do it for us.

The etheric body is also a mold, a blueprint of our body. Filling it with energy is enough for it to revitalize the cells that need it because it already knows the structure of your physical body.

If you have been following the instructions, at this moment you have done at least seven days of candle training and the next exercise will work for you. If not, stop reading and do the candle exercise, then come back after seven days.

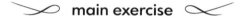 main exercise

Energetic balls exercise

Time and duration
After the morning candle exercise, for as long as it takes (normally around 10–15 minutes).

What to do
"Compress" the *prana*, the energy that is in the air, and roll it over the body.

How to do it
After the morning candle; or if you don't have the option to do it in the morning, you can do it in any other free time, but you must perform the candle exercise first.

Stand up, rub the palms together to heat them a bit. Feel or imagine the energetic flow moving in your hands and palms. Make slow movements with the hands, keeping your attention on the palms. Feel as if your palm is touching a ball of water. Remember, in a pool or at the seaside, the sensation when you put your opened palm lightly on the water? This is the feeling we are looking for.

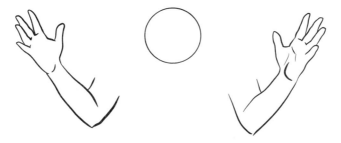

When you think you feel it (trust yourself) hold both palms in front of your heart. With your intention, create a ball of energy with your palms by compressing the energy in the air (prana). Keep doing this until you feel the edges of the ball. It will look like you are clapping but without the palms touching. Your hands and palms must be completely relaxed. If you tense the body you stop the energy flow.

The key here is to work with both the hands and the intention. You have to trust yourself and, if something doesn't work, don't lose faith. The ability is in you and you just have to tune yourself to it.

You will not be able to make the ball if you do not yet feel the effect from the morning candle exercise. This is fine; for now just keep moving the palms slowly, looking for the feeling of "touching water" or other feelings on your palms. And keep going with the morning candle; the more you work with it, the better you will be able to feel and move energies.

—

For some people this exercise will be easy and they will make the ball right away; others have to keep doing the candle exercises and this one until they can make and feel the edges of the ball. We will elaborate later on the exercises' principles, but here is one tip: we all have some people who we resonate well with. Our lower chakras produce the most basic and common-to-all feeling that illustrates the law of resonance. (Normally, when we feel sexual attraction, one of our most primal feelings, it is due to lower-chakras resonance.) So we will succeed in this and other exercises when we do them with people with whom we resonate well on the energetic level. Everyone around you either helps you, drags you down or does nothing either way. We have to surround ourselves with the first kind. There are some people whose presence makes your energy flow better, and performing the exercises near them or, better, with them will be much easier and faster (and it will be the opposite with people who have energetic dissonance with you). Nothing has to be hard. Spiritual development and everything related is simple and easy.

—

After making the ball, hold it on your palm with the palm facing the sky (upwards). Now put it on the other palm. Feel the energy on your palm and keep your attention on the ball. You can smile if it feels natural to you. Move the ball from palm to palm another few times. If you lose it, make a new one. It is totally normal to lose the ball; it happens if your attention has moved, your energetic bodies have absorbed the ball or your inner attention is not strong enough yet.

When you feel confident enough, start moving the ball using the other hand, touch by touch, up from your palm in the direction of the shoulder. The ball has to stay on the hand as if you are moving a real ball that is rolling up your arm from the palm to the shoulder. Then roll it behind the neck to the other shoulder, switch hands, and keep rolling it down to the other palm, and then back to the original palm.

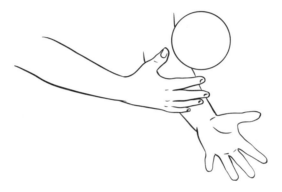

Moving the ball from one palm to the other and back counts as one time. Do it ten times. This sounds a lot and long, but it is nothing of the sort. Once you are able to make the ball and roll it, the whole thing won't take more than 5–7 minutes.

When you have done it ten times on the hands, put the ball on the upper side of one foot. Roll it up with the counter-hand (left for the right foot and right for the left) up to the lap, under the navel, switch hands, and roll it down to the upper side of the other foot. Then roll it back to the original foot. Again, rolling it there and back counts as one time. Do it ten times.

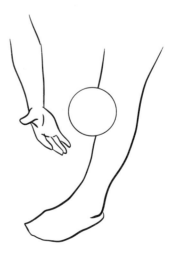

Then, make one big ball and hold it with both hands. Move it back and forth on your lap, like your hands are the ropes of a swings and the ball is the swing. Keep your concentration on the ball and the areas of the body it touches. Five times, then stop the ball inside the body, while your hands are parallel to the body, and begin moving the ball up inside your body until you raise it above your head, and back down to its original position. Five times.

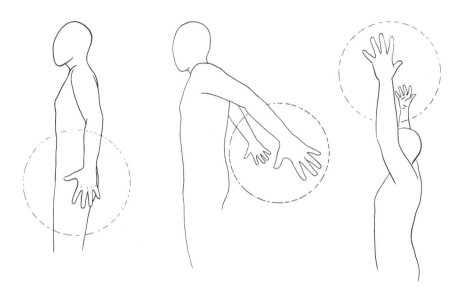

Try to feel the energies of the balls and the body. Observe if the ball goes willingly in some places and gets stuck in others. Let the ball lead, don't push or force it. If it gets stuck it indicates a blockage. Relax the area. Use your intention to relax. If this is difficult, use your breathing. Don't rush the process.

If something does not work, or you have done it for fewer times than advised, and you are unable to make new balls, you are done for today. Come back to the exercise tomorrow.

What not to do
- Don't create any distractions around yourself (music, TV, etc.); keep your attention on the balls.

- Don't move the ball with anything but your hand(s); try to disengage your thoughts.
- Don't move the ball anywhere but the route described.

How and when do I know it's working?

When you have the feelings, when you feel the balls and the contact with the ball, you know it is working. Especially when you manage to do the whole exercise with one ball, fast and easily.

Why am I doing it?

You are helping your etheric body to gain its vitality, helping the channels in the body to open up and renewing the flow of the energy. You are helping the energy to reach every cell of your body. You are developing your sensitivity in the right way. And of course, you're doing it for fun.

In short

Use *prana*, in the form of an energetic ball, to revitalize the etheric body.

 complementary exercises

The wheel of power or small wheel

Time and duration

Any time. Takes a few minutes.

What to do

Compress an energetic ball and send it to circulate in the body.

How to do it

Some quick theoretical background: we have two important channels (meridians) that originate low in the body, between the legs (lower pelvis, crotch). There is one at the front and one at the back. They start from the same place but never meet or close the circle. Thus, these channels are not operational most of the time. The reason why they do not close the circle is their ending points. One (the front one) ends under the lower lip and the other (the back one) ends in the niche between the nose and the upper lip. Both channels run a finger or two's depth from the surface of the skin. We can close the circle by touching the hard palate with the tongue.

Let's begin. Place your tongue on the top of your mouth (hard palate) or just fold it in a way that it touches both the bottom and the top part of the mouth. Heat the palms by rubbing them together. Make an energetic ball and compress it to tennis-ball size or even a bit smaller. As you compress it, imagine that it changes color to red. Through the lower *dan tian* (around two to three finger-widths under the navel—use intuition), insert the ball into your body and with intention ask it to go to the lower part of the spine, to the coccyx.

Imagine a person you love and who loves you, who is or was close to you (the difference between imagination and mind action is the presence of intentions, so imagine intentionally). Feel the love between you. This person is touching the ball with their finger and moving it slowly up the spine. Meanwhile you inhale. When the ball reaches the crown of the head (feel it charging with golden universal energy), it goes down, passing the tongue, and lower, to its original place (where it charges from the Earthly silver energy). From the top of the head down, exhale. The movement of the ball is done entirely by the finger of the person you're imagining, who loves you and who you love (if you have difficulties thinking in terms of love, then think of respect, gratitude or care). In short, the person uses their finger to move the ball up the spine, to the top of the head, via the tongue and down to the starting place. At the top there is a golden

46

energy charge, at the bottom a silver energy charge. While the ball is moving it releases the energy it gets from the universe and from Earth into the body and the channel.

—

Later, you will do this exercise without the help of the person you love. Use your breathing in synchronicity with the direction of the ball. Inhale up the spine to the top of the head. Exhale down to the origin of the channel. Since at the beginning the ball moves slowly, it is okay to take more than one inhale for the upwards movement and more than one exhale for the downwards. Later, when the ball will start to move faster, you can adjust its speed to one deep inhale and exhale. Let the energies open the channels and fill your body with vitality. See the golden and the silver colors as light circulating in the channels.

The number of the times the ball has to make a full circle is a multiplication of nine. But I leave you to experience and experiment. As long as the number of repetitions is a bit higher than enough to open the channels.

After fulfilling the first whole circle, let the person make another two circles, keeping your attention on the ball and not forgetting to breathe accordingly. The fourth time (if you feel confident), let the person release their touch on the ball, and keep moving it with your intention (keep breathing). It is okay if the first few times you do this exercise all the movements are done by the other person; this channel might have been closed for quite a while. When you feel that the time has come, release the other person and move the ball using your intention.

—

Now create a new ball and do everything from the beginning; only this time the ball runs along the front channel, passing the tongue, to the top of the head and down the spine. Keep breathing: on the up, inhale and on the down, exhale.

Try to keep the back straight, hands on the navel: women left hand on top, men right hand on top. Closed mouth and eyes; and breathe through the nose.

This exercise can take various forms. The starting point can be different; some people perform it starting from the top of the head. They visualize the seventh chakra with a golden ball that goes down. This is also fine; but here we begin from the root, so red it is. The number of circles can be is different; and in some versions there is no loving person.

For those who are interested in the names of the channels: *Ren Mai* (任脉) is the front channel, and *Du Mai* (督脉) is the back channel. The point at the top of the head is *Bai Hui* (百会) and the lower point in the crotch (When we stand straight and upright, the upper one is exactly above the lower one) is called *Hui Yin* (会阴).

What not to do
- Keep the tongue touching the roof of the mouth throughout.
- In some places, it will seem like the ball is moving aside or jumping; those are the blockages. Be more persistent until the ball passes through them. Use love and not force.

How and when do I know it's working?
You will feel clarity in your head (after a while), energetic and physical comfort, and energy circulation.

Why am I doing it?
Energetic circulation is part of vitality, health and self-fulfillment. You help your upper and lower energetic centers wake up and synchronize. If the energy does not move, we can get ill.

In short
Help your energetic centers to wake up and synchronize through energetic circulation of the small wheel.

Tai Chi standing posture
(or any other martial art)

Time and duration
Every day for a minimum of 20 minutes.

What to do
Stand, relax and let energy flow through the body.

How to do it
The martial arts standing posture is very basic and simple but one cannot overexaggerate its importance and effectiveness. The performance of standing is relatively easy, and even the act of finding the right position is simple and with time and experience becomes automatic. The hard part is to keep standing regardless of the discomfort of the body, mind and emotions.

This exercise combines physical shape with the importance of complete relaxation. We have already spoken of the etheric body and looked at how we change its shape with our actions (suck it in). When we have pain and tense the spot where we feel the pain, we stop the flow of the energy (when we tense the physical body we tense the energetic bodies).

In some cases, the pain is almost chronic and so we may be almost permanently tensed. So relaxation with the right actions will bring back the flow of the energy. This exercise will help us to gain the new, healthy habits of a relaxed body and constant energy flow.

The whole exercise is to stand and do nothing. This doing nothing releases us from wasting energy and removes all the obstacles that block the flow of energy through our bodies between the universe and Earth. As babies, we were completely relaxed. It was less efficient, because the energy flows even better when we are relaxed and standing with the spine straight; but the energy, nonetheless, was flowing. Today, most of us cannot relax even when going to bed. Performing this exercise will remind you and your body how it feels to be relaxed again.

The key elements are posture, breathing, awareness and tongue touching the hard palate. The posture goes like this: put your tongue up, have the feet shoulder-width apart parallel to each other, and then open them a bit to the sides (the ankles don't move). Rise up a little by folding your toes under the feet, like you are trying to hold the ground with them. Imagine that you have helium in your head, or that something is pulling your head up from the top. Feel how your spine is stretching up and your neck, chest and lower back vertebrae take their natural place. Feel how you become a bit taller.

Now bend the knees a bit and move the pelvis forward. If you put your hand on your lower back, you will feel how it becomes flat or straight. Take your chest just a bit back (like you are sucking it in), and the chin just a bit down. Here you have it. In the complete version of the posture exercise we raise our hands to the level of the upper chest as though we were holding a big barrel or something round. Then we imagine holding two balls: one between the legs and one in the hands (with the one in the hands, imagine the part that touches your chest is pushing into you, making you concave the chest a bit by bringing the shoulders slightly forward). But in our version of the exercise the hands-up part can be skipped. If you do want to do it, do it with the hands up.

⁓

You need to feel relaxed in this posture, so if there is any kind of discomfort, play with the body to find comfort. It should feel like the upper part of the body sits on the lower one lightly and effortlessly. Breathe calmly from the belly and be absolutely relaxed. If you feel discomfort or pain, direct your calmness and the warm energy to the place of pain (or move the part that is in pain). Your awareness has to be present and to observe the processes that are happening in your bodies under the influence of the energetic flow. Be here and now. Don't let your thoughts take you away. And last but not least, keep your tongue on the hard palate. This is very important.

At the end of the exercise, raise your hands above your head and imagine (with intention) that you are holding a golden ball of *prana*. Take your hands down, letting the ball of *prana* pass through your body, and release it to the center of the planet. Do it three times. Then put your palms under the navel (the lower *dan tian*), men right hand on top, women left hand. Visualize the *dan tian* as a ball of fire, like an iron ball of steel after it's been taken out of the fire. The centers of the palms stay one on top of the other on top of the *dan tian*. Close your eyes, and stay that way for a few minutes. Visualize the *dan tian* hot, or even burning.

⁓

This posture is all about a straight back. Straight in the geometrical sense, like a straight line. The idea behind this posture and exercise is that we have three important energetic centers in our body called *dan tian* (丹田) or in the yogic traditions, *bindu*. The top one is in the

51

head, the middle one is under the chest and the lower one is under the navel (for the exact locations use your intuition). When those three centers are aligned, the body is relaxed and breathing is calm, the flow of the cosmic energy is at its most efficient.

The benefits of this exercise could fill a whole book. Just standing like that could cure any disease. It allows you to connect yourself to nature, to Earth and the universe. In martial arts it means to grow strong roots. It balances and opens every channel, every meridian and every energetic center. At some levels of consciousness, it even cleanses your karma; the emotional discomfort, although it feels like hell sometimes, does the cleansing.

If you are healthy, it is enough to stand for around 20–30 minutes a day (For optimal results, though, try one hour every day). And if you have particular problems or energetic deficiency you would like to cure, stand for longer.

What not to do
- Don't let your brain wander; be here and now.
- Don't hold the breath; pay attention as you breathe.
- Don't play music or watch TV.
- If you feel blockages or discomfort it is fine, it means the energy is cleansing the channels; don't stop, keep going.

How and when do I know it's working?
This depends on the condition of your body, particularly on if you have already been practicing yoga, qigong or any other energetic practice; on the condition of your energetic and physical bodies; and sometimes on the geographical area you're in; there are some specific places with strong energy, and more generally, villages or quiet rural areas, and places with water sources like rivers or the sea nearby, or mountains, are better than cities. Normally, to feel the first effects takes a few months. With time, you will feel that your body is more solid, as if your energetic bodies have become

denser. Your physical movements will feel more flowing. The effect cannot be taken away. The more you invest in standing the more you gain.

Why am I doing it?
Balance, health, self-esteem, energetic potential and conductivity. To learn to experience the flow of energy and its impact on you.

In short
Simply standing like this with a straight back, breathing naturally from the belly, lets energy flow through the body and its value cannot be overstated.

Etheric hands

Time and duration
No specific time. Do it for a couple of minutes.

What to do
Keeping your physical hands still, lift your energetic hands outside the physical hands.

How to do it
Wash your physical hands with the coldest water you can get from your tap (the colder the better) from above the elbows down to the tips of the fingers. Find a comfortable place and sit. Put your physical hands on the upper belly, so the solar plexus is between them. Palms down, fingers separated, hands very close to but not touching each other.

Take a deep breath and hold it just long enough so you can release the air slowly and calmly. Do this three times. You will see that every time you can inhale more, keep it longer, and release slower. If you know how to breathe with full yogic breath, even better.

Close your eyes and breathe calmly. Let the body breathe; you are just an observer at the moment. When you feel ready (use intuition), imagine with intention raising your energetic left hand out of the physical left hand. Your physical hand remains still and calm; only the energetic double rises. Lower it back down. Do the same with the right hand. Do it slowly.

Open your eyes and, with intention, take both left and right hands out and touch the floor (or the sofa or anything else). From what you touch with the energetic hands, feel the texture and the feeling on the physical hands. Touch your head, feet and face. Enter the physical body with the energetic body on your most sensitive spot (normally a part of the back or the feet), move it inside and take it out. Play and experiment with your energetic hands as much as you like. Keep in mind that when you work with energetic bodies your concentration should be on the energetic level, not the physical one. Try not to concentrate on the physical aspect; stay subtle. Return the hands back.

What not to do
- Don't touch living creatures without their permission.
- Don't leave your hands inside your body for too long.
- Don't forget to return the energetic hands back to the physical.

How and when do I know it's working?
When you can feel with your physical hands whatever the energetic hands do, it is a good indication that it's working. Feeling pins and needles in the palms of the physical hands after a while is also an indicator that your energetic hands are out of the physical.

This exercise may seem paranormal but in reality it is very natural. When you move your body, you move all the energetic bodies and the physical at once (just as when you tense the physical body you tense the energetic bodies). To move the energetic body only, you just leave the physical to rest. In your mind, in your feelings, everything is absolutely the same as the process of moving the physical body.

Why am I doing it?
Strengthening your etheric body, learning about the structure of the bodies from practice and not only from theory. Exploring the energetic potential and conductivity of the hands and building the basics for more complicated and fun etheric hands exercises.

In short
We learn to operate our energetic hands as a part of broadening our consciousness and getting to know our abilities.

Emotional Body

The spirit is able to experience emotions. What makes it possible is the subtle matter (conductor) called the emotional body. Emotions are a common thing between us and the animals. From this point of view, emotions are an animalistic part of our nature and we must learn to use them appropriately—or master them.

Emotions are not chaotic, not shallow and not animalistic (per se). We can say that they were "introduced" to us by the animals, but they exist in more dimensions than our physical eyes see. Thus, emotions bring us energies from higher realms, higher dimensions. In some ways, in the heavy matter in which we live, it is only possible for us to operate thanks to them. You won't be able to get out of bed if you don't have a reason; and behind a reason stands the emotion. No emotions, no energies. Of course emotions are not the only source of energy, but they are definitely one of the strongest.

Emotions can be used as fuel, but before using a certain emotion in this way one must practice for a long time, starting from getting to know your emotional world better. For that we have to separate the emotion from our "natural" reaction. We, at current stages, stay on the level of reducing negative emotions and maximizing positive ones.

Every emotion has its chakra (energetic center) and organ that it relates to. When we are experiencing the emotion, the energy is passing (flowing) through the relevant chakra and organ. Imbalanced emotion will lead to problems in the energetic center it corresponds with: the chakra or the organ, or both.

Emotions are ways and channels of experiencing creation, the world around us. They are like thoughts, but at a lower vibration. We are able to think, through either an active or reactive process. Thought is a way to experience creation, normally by *understanding*. You hold a book, this idea of a book resonates in your mind as the *thought* of the book and in your emotional body as a feeling of the book (we have emotional feedback on thoughts). Our perception of reality on the mental level comes from an energy form we call thought, and, on the emotional level, from emotions or feelings.

Emotions and thoughts are important for us to be able to operate in physical reality. When emotions and thoughts are balanced we can develop intuition. Intuition is important for higher realms and is also very useful in the physical world. We can operate here without intuition but we cannot without mind and emotions.

Emotions are passive, emotions can be provoked and controlled. Emotions are dynamic, they are in motion, they are energetic gates.

They can be suppressed or boosted, they have peaks and troughs. Emotions are teachers, but only after learning and balancing the emotion can we consider the lesson learned.

Emotions are neither good nor bad; but misuse of emotions that leads to imbalance is bad. Emotions are just a tool. If you hit yourself on the finger with a hammer, the hammer is not responsible or bad. It is about you. It's the same with emotions; don't blame them, observe them without judging, learn.

Every kind of energy we experience or create resonates at a certain frequency. We can say that the frequency is what gives matter its characteristics. There are no good or bad frequencies, and there are no good or bad emotions. High frequencies does not mean good and low does not mean bad. Some emotions have low vibrations but it does not mean they are bad. Every emotion has reason, although sometimes we can hardly see it because we are overwhelmed and reactive. But when we look back or balance the emotion we can see the logic and the lesson it brings.

If we look carefully we will see that there is no such thing as time in the notion we imagine, there is only rhythm (physicists won't agree with me). If we look at space (not outer space, but space as in a room) as a dimension, we can see that we can travel everywhere in three dimensions. For us space is not a limited dimension. But since we cannot move in the dimension of time in every direction we want, it seems like time is limited for us. From here we have the perception of the flowing of time (moments in the past and the moments that are yet to come); the feeling that it flows in one direction and we cannot go back (at least not physically). If hypothetically we could see time from outside like we can see space, the perception of time as we know it would become irrelevant. In other words, time is relevant when you have to be at work at nine a.m. but irrelevant for your spiritual existence.

As for rhythm, we have dualities (polarities): hot/cold, day/night, joy/sadness. The rhythm shows us the frequency at which two polarities change places and take effect. Normally, the polarities have opposite vibrations. If joy vibrates high, sadness will vibrate low. The vibrations move from lower to higher and back to lower and back to higher and so one.

We cannot reach high vibrations without being at the lower first. Our lower vibrations are the starting point. There we "make" the space for future creations. Just as, when we study, the material has to move from short-term to long-term memory to create emptiness in the short-term memory. When we feel overwhelmed with information we rest. Action is high vibration, rest is low vibration. We started with a blank mind (low vibration), took the action of studying (high vibration) and switched to resting (to regain the emptiness of the low vibration again). None of these states is good or bad but the cyclic change of them is the right thing, is healthy.

I will try to illustrate it with an emotional example: joy and sadness. We feel joy from an action that is connected to creativity, creativity that resonates with our wishes. The flow of joy is in place as long as you are in the process of fulfilling the creational potential; when you fulfill your destiny that you chose for yourself. When creational potential is fulfilled, the flow of joy stops, we feel full and cannot keep creating (no energy, no creation). When the whole process of creation is over and we feel full, or satisfied, we have to let sadness complete the cycle and replace joy. After sadness is over, we are ready for a new creational impulse (sometimes the sadness is not there, but the emptiness must be).

When we finish a period in our life or move from one workplace or home to another we feel sadness for exactly this reason. Here is your secret of creation—if you are an artist, your muse: look for the sadness or emptiness after the peak.

Summer is hot, and is the time of high vibrations. Peak agricultural season. We expend a lot of energy and experience "positive" emotions. What comes after the summer? And what are the emotions that come with it? I think you know the answer.

So emotions have polarities, triggers and rhythm (the frequency of switching between polarities). It is important to point out that most people don't reach the peak of the potential of the energy. One thing is for sure: the feedback from the high emotion will end up with the depth of the low emotion at the same scale. This is the law of pendulum.

There is another thing we must know about emotions. When we are kids or in a state where we are connected to ourselves (I will talk later about how to achieve this state), we climb easily from low to high emotions. But now, we have to put extra effort into lifting ourselves from the low vibrations, most of the time unsuccessfully. So in the "ordinary" conditions of our lives we go to lower emotions easily but raise to higher only with great effort, if at all.

Emotions are channels of energy that help us to operate in the heavy matter called the physical world. The right balance between the emotions helps us develop in a healthy way. By "develop" I mean in every aspect of life. Development comes through experience, from actions, from try and fail, develop, release, gain emptiness and develop the next. But only as long as we are developing the *right things* can we count on high emotions to come to our rescue and bring us back up. The right things are the one that resonate with our wishes with joy.

As most people don't live in balance, they have energetic deficiency. To compensate for this deficiency, people "steal" energy from each other. There are quite a few ways of doing it and everyone has their own strategy. People can be divided into two categories: energetic predators and energetic prey (most of the sensitives fall into the second category).

Attention is energy; we "feed" what we pay our attention to. People who need our attention constantly (e.g., by guilt-tripping us into giving it) "drink" our energies. Reflect: who always catches you and involves you in a long conversation from which you cannot escape?

Sexual attention. Do you know people who tease and flirt but never give? Attracting your attention through sexually charged means. Sexual energy is the most vital for creation and stable life. These people tend to surround themselves with "potential" sex partners—friends who are attracted to them—while friend-zoning them, keeping their interest alive and enjoying the attention and sexual attraction. They like to feel wanted and keep the people who want them close (but not too close) so they can feed from their energy.

Pity (as opposed to compassion) is a very good tool for the "weak" to take your energy. Pity makes you the subject of pity. If we pity the person who is sick, the energy of that sickness is transferred to us. If we pity someone for being disappointed, the energy and sometimes the feelings will be transferred to us. How many times have you been there for someone who has elicited pity, whether through a situation, pain or heavy emotion, who has "dumped" their undesirable energy on you? Think of how people who you pity feel relieved after a conversation with you. You might think that you are a magical person who cures everyone by your close attention; that you are a good listener, emotionally involved.

Anger is a powerful emotion that tends to escalate. People using this strategy to steal energies look to provoke others into experiencing anger or engaging in a verbal fight.

Other ways of wasting energy are: people I cannot forgive (including myself), people whose approval I am seeking (or people whose judgement I'm afraid of) and situations and people whom I seek to control (kids, work subordinates and others).

In addition to the nature of the emotions discussed above, there are emotional "malfunctions," popularly known as emotional traumas, which happens when the emotion is stuck in a loop and is provoked based on previous negative experiences. When consciousness is witnessing a situation it marks the situation with a tag. It goes like this: you see something, you interpret it; meanwhile the appropriate emotion to your *interpretation* comes up and lodges in the memory. From now on, this energetic combination will influence your life until you can untie the combination and release the energy.

This aspect is well known and I have nothing new to contribute here. However, methods of uniting the energies and releasing the traumas will be described later on. Just, please, be patient and don't jump there right away. The book is built in such a way that every exercise prepares you to be able to perform the next one. You don't yet have the tools.

As described in astrology, stars have a certain influence on us. The influence of the stars works only on an emotional level. The stars can give their energies to a specific emotion or set of emotions; emotions as cosmic energies. Remember we said that emotions are energetic gates. On some days some of us are very easily provoked to anger and on other days we could not be more indifferent to the world around us.

Those energies of emotions have to be mastered as a part of reaching balance. A balanced person who manages emotions well can be above the stars in the sense that the emotions cannot dictate to them how to live, how to react. Animals react automatically in this way; and many of us are the same. But when we don't react automatically, when we control the gates of energy that we call emotions, we leave behind the animalistic realm of emotions and the influence of the stars.

In our physical world, we feel and act like we are individual beings, separate from each other. In reality, even if we can't see how exactly, we all are interconnected. We can say that everything around us is a mirror, a reflection of our inner world. Everything that we have inside us, on all the levels, we have outside (like the shared subconsciousness—yes, we all have one subconsciousness we share, like a field that connects us all).

The Law of Correspondence—or "as above so below, as within so without . . ."—means that every time you feel or experience an emotion towards another person, thing, or idea outside you, there is something inside you that corresponds with the other. In normal human language, this is to say that when you hate something and express it, it impacts you as well.

For example if you hate a classmate, that energy of hatred impacts the classmate but also you; the same "wishes" we send to others are directed automatically to ourselves as well. When people say if you do harm to others you harm yourself, it is not only karma they mean (or that God will punish you); it is about you literally harming yourself.

The good news is that on the same principle, expressing positive emotions reflects back on us. So the more you express or experience Love, Happiness, Joy, Gratitude, Generosity, the better you do for yourself.

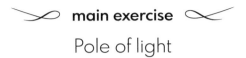

main exercise

Pole of light

Time and duration
Every day, 10–20 minutes.

What to do
Stand in a pole of light and enjoy it.

How to do it
Stand comfortably, legs shoulder-width apart or more, as is comfortable for you. If you have been practicing doing the standing posture, you can put your back in a straight line as you have learned to. The posture has to be comfortable so you will be able to relax completely. After taking this posture, relaxing and breathing calmly, eyes closed, visualize a pole of light coming from the center of the universe to the center of Earth. Its width is as wide as the width of your hands when you spread them out at your sides. This light is passing through you and your body is in the center of it.

This pole channels universal energy to Earth and Earth energy back to the universe. The energy that comes from the center of the universe is golden and the energy that goes back is silver. When the pole is well established, raise your hands and hug it; bring it a bit closer to you. Leave your hands in the air, level with your chest, with the palms towards the chest (like when you hug someone). The hands make the shape of a circle but are not connected.

As you stand in the middle of the circle, feel the energies going around and through you. Those energies are protecting you, cleansing all your bodies and healing all the wounds and illnesses. Feel how it takes away all that is unhealthy and unnecessary, bringing instead energy, health and calmness. Keep your concentration on the pole.

Observe and feel it, live with it. This is a natural pole of energy that you are a channel for.

After a few minutes of standing and hugging the pole of light, feel gratitude towards the pole. Thank it. Keep the good feeling of it. Now slowly let the hands go down towards the lower *dan tian* (two to three fingers under the navel). Put the palms on the *dan tian* with the centers of the palms exactly on it, women left hand on top, men right hand on top. And let the good feeling and good vibrations be absorbed by the body and resonate with the energies of the pole.

At the end, don't forget to turn the pole off.

What not to do

Don't use it to protect anyone who hasn't given their permission. The exception is your kids when they are very young; at an age when you still make decisions for them.

How and when do I know it's working?

If you feel a good feeling of calmness and protection that is covering your whole body, it is working.

Why am I doing it?

This is a natural pole of energy. You are a magnet and an energetic channel. You let energies flow through your bodies, energies that exchange between Earth and the universe. When this stream of energies is strong and stable it is the best protection for all your bodies, feelings and emotions (and your mind, of course). While meditating on the pole, visualizing it, we make it stronger and more active. When the pole is in place and strong we have noth ing to be afraid of from the energetic point of view. No one and nothing can harm us.

In short

Learn how to stand comfortably, locate the *dan tian*, see the pole of light, and let it help you be happy.

complementary exercises
Turning off the field of senses

Time and duration
The first time, it might take up to 20 minutes. Later, with training, it will work in a split-second.

What to do
Enter a trance mode and turn off the field of senses.

How to do it
It is more of an experiment than an exercise; you don't need to repeat it. The only thing that could be considered an exercise is going into a trance state.

The level of success depends on how deep is the state of trance and how strong is your will.

Your sitting posture in meditation is important. Advanced yogis (or simply flexible people) can sit in the lotus posture (*padmasana*), but half-lotus (*ardha padmasana*) or accomplished pose (*siddhasana*, also known as adept's pose) are also absolutely fine; you just need to be able to relax completely and keep your back straight. If this is still difficult, feel free to put something comfortable under your bottom (like a firm cushion or folded blanket). The object can be as high as necessary for you to effortlessly keep your back straight.

Sit in a comfortable position. Take a deep breath, hold it for a few seconds and then exhale slowly. Repeat three times. Create the pole of light from the previous exercise for protection. Start moving in a circle, from the loins up, like the top of your head is drawing circles on the ceiling. Start your "drawing" by moving to the left. In yoga we exhale every time we go in and inhale every time we go out. This movement is going in, so before starting the movement, inhale, then begin moving and exhaling in such a way that when you reach the middle of the circle you finish exhaling. From the middle, draw the circle to the right and inhale. When you return to your starting point, you should have finished inhaling. Move slowly and try to synchronize movement and breathing.

Draw seven circles in one direction and seven in the other. You should be calm, feel like you are sinking in your mind into a meditative, sleepy mode.

On the last circle, stop when you reach the center, breathe and slowly exhale, then move back to your original position in a straight line (so this time you draw a half-circle). Meanwhile, feel how you sink even deeper into a meditative state. If you feel like the outer reality seems far off, you have reached this state.

Now see yourself in a small room. See yourself as in reality, not from outside; looking out from your own head and seeing the world through your eyes. On the wall across from you, there is a light switch, with a red button, and the light is on and it's red. When you turn it off, your field of sensitivity will shrink back to your chest area and you will feel nothing from outside. Now turn it back on, see the red light on again and feel the field of sensitivity taking its original place, coming out of your chest and spreading back around your bodies.

Turn to the left wall and see a volume button turned to maximum. Turn it down a bit and feel how the field is shrinking; move it all the way down and feel how the field has completely shrunk into the chest. Move it back up, to its original position.

Direct your attention to the body. Observe its natural breathing. Feel the clothes on your skin and your surroundings; that your presence (awareness) is coming back to the physical world. Feel how your consciousness is climbing up, back to reality. If you feel difficulties coming back, don't panic; think of something logical like math. You could think of a simple addition or subtraction, or of a puzzle; your brain, moving to beta waves, will bring you out of the trance very fast.

Turn off the pole of light.

What not to do
- Don't forget to turn the field of protection off.
- Don't stay in trance after finishing, come back to reality.

How and when do I know it's working?
You will know.

Why am I doing it?
To understand the nature of things, to practice different ways of accessing trance state and the field of sensitivity that I imagine you have guessed to be your energetic bodies' fields. It is up to you, but you have to know that when you turn the field off, you turn off part of your protection. It is because in the beginning we cannot separate the actual element of informational feedback we call sensitivity from the rest of the energetic fields. But once we can, we are able to turn off or balance just the sensitivity.

In short
Practice accessing and using trance state to help you understand the nature of things.

Turning off all the unnecessary things that you pay attention to

Time and duration

This exercise is performed just once, but you can revisit it as and when you feel it necessary. Duration is around 20 minutes.

What to do

Sit, go to trance, go to your room from the previous exercise. and turn off your attention from all the things that do not serve you.

How to do it

Enter trance using the same method as in the previous exercise, sitting and turning in circles. Put on the same protections (you will again turn them off at the end). Go to the same room. As in the previous exercise, the level of success, its efficiency, depends on the quality of the trance state and willpower.

The difference is that now when you are in the room, you turn to the left wall and see a light switch with a green light. Now, have in mind that from the second you turn it off, everything around you, in and out, that catches your attention and does not serve you will stop attracting your attention. You will stop noticing everything that does not serve your path in life.

When my teacher helped me through this exercise, when he said, "Now you won't notice everything that is not serving your path," 90 per cent of what I was feeling with all my sensitivity just disappeared, like it was never there to begin with; like how a pain leaves you after you take a pill.

This exercise, like the previous one, is more of an experiment. You decide if you want to turn things off permanently or not.

A reminder: when you get out of the trance, turn off the pole of light.

What not to do

Don't stay in trance.

How and when do I know it's working?

Things that you have been sensing will disappear from your radar.

Why am I doing it?

From the moment we discover that we sense a lot, we develop curiosity towards everything around us. We, like kids, stick our noses in everywhere. But at some point, our curiosity will be fulfilled and we will have learned everything we wanted to— from the point of view of the senses. But as a sensitive person, we tend to "explore" everything around us through sensitivity; our whole range of sensitivity is open. We still feel everything as if we have just encountered reality or discovered our sensitivity for the first time.

So, this is the time to put an end to sensing unnecessary and unrelated things. You will still feel everything you want by directing your attention to it, but you will stop feeling things that your attention did not intend to be aware of.

In short

Sit, go to trance, turn off unnecessary things from your radar and come back.

Note: Now you know that you are in control of your sensitivity and your senses. Another small thing that is important to note: when you look at something you get so-called feedback that delivers the information about the object you are looking at into your energetic system. This is because with just an ordinary look, glance, we direct one energetic "octopus arm" to the object of our curiosity.

Take your time and practice looking without sending out any "arms" or expecting any feedback. When you look at something, tell yourself: "I am just looking and seeing, nothing to sense. Just looking . . ."

Balancing feminine and masculine energies
Nadi Shodhana Pranayama
(alternative breathing or alternate nostril breathing)

Time and duration
It is good to do it every day, twice a day, morning and evening.
Duration 5–10 minutes a time.

What to do
Sit comfortably, back straight. Using your fingers, close one of the nostrils while breathing from the other, then switch nostrils.

How to do it
Sit comfortably with the back straight. Place your left hand on the leg or in the lap, with the palm open towards the sky (alternatively you can use the *chinmaya* or *gyan mudra*). With your right hand make the Jesus *mudra* (index and middle fingers are together and straight, ring and pinky together but folded). Place the middle finger on the space between the eyebrows. Your thumb falls on the right nostril and the two folded fingers on the left.

And here we go: starting with the left nostril (meaning the right one is closed by the thumb), inhale through the left; close it, opening the right nostril, and exhale. Inhale through the right, close it, and exhale through the left. This is one round.

We always start and finish breathing with the left nostril. And we don't inhale and exhale with the same nostril at one time. The one we inhale with is not the one we exhale with. You've got it. Keep your attention on the breathing process.

The inhale and the exhale should be equal in duration. You can measure this in seconds or by heartbeats (heartbeats is better, because they represent our inner "flowing" natural rhythm, while the clock represents a random "constant" rhythm). Your inhale and exhale should be of the same duration. You can start with three rounds and work up to seven or nine.

What not to do

- Don't breathe in an arrhythmic way; the inhale should be equal to the exhale.
- Don't finish on the right nostril.
- Don't stop until you have reached the natural end of the exercise.

How and when do I know it's working?

It is very subtle work; not many people can feel the differences when they are actually happening. But over time you will be calmer and more balanced.

Why am I doing it?

To balance the polar energies in the energetic bodies. Breathing is the way of life (inhale) and death (exhale) and has to be balanced. In addition, there are two energetic channels on each side of the body. Those channels end in the nostrils, and each nostril is responsible for each channel. Breathing in this way helps to open and balance each channel and balance the channels between themselves.

In short

Balance the feminine and the masculine energies through rhythmical breathing using one nostril at a time.

Balancing feminine and masculine energies
Anjali Mudra

Time and duration
7–10 minutes, twice a day, morning and evening.

What to do
Sit with a straight back, put your palms together, thumbs closed towards the palms, as in the Namaste greeting.

How to do it
Sit comfortably with the back straight. Put the palms together in the Indian "thank you" manner *(anjali mudra)*. Place this *mudra* on the level of the heart, touching the chest with the thumbs. You can lower the head slightly.

This is very simple to perform, as you can see. Keep your attention on the *mudra*.

What not to do
- Don't have distractions like TV or music, or anything else that might pull your attention away from the exercise.
- Don't let the flowing mind take over.

How and when do I know it's working?
Like the previous exercise, this one works on a subtle level and many people don't actually feel the effect right away. Over time, though, your inner polar energies will be balanced.

Why am I doing it?
Balancing the polar energies in the energetic bodies; balancing the right and the left sides of the bodies.

In short

Balance the feminine and the masculine energies through taking a *mudra*, with your palms together at the level of the heart.

Balancing feminine and masculine energies
Equal-Armed Cross

Time and duration

10–15 minutes in the morning.

What to do

Relax and visualize an equal-armed cross.

How to do it

Take a comfortable sitting position, put protection in with the pole of light and gradually relax completely. Feel how every part of your body becomes relaxed and heavy. Feel how the more you relax the less you feel the physical body. When you are completely relaxed, feel how your consciousness is sliding down, like falling asleep.

After reaching the trance state of the mind, imagine an equal-armed cross. Its horizontal arm symbolizes the feminine energies and the vertical the masculine energies. See how perfect the cross is, how the arms are equal in size and meet in the exact middle. This symbolizes the perfect balance between the energies of the feminine and the masculine.

When you feel ready, let the inner balance and integrity of the cross be projected; let it influence your masculine and feminine energies, putting them into a perfect balance like those of the cross. Feel how your inner energies come into balance.

The deeper you are in the meditative or trance state, the better and longer-lasting will be the results.

Come out of trance gradually by switching your attention from inner to outer (from your inner experiences to physical objects in the room). Pay attention to your breathing and surroundings. Feel how your consciousness is going back up to its original place.

Remove the protections.

What not to do

Don't do more than given in the exercise. Your relationship with the cross has to be exactly as described.

How and when do I know it's working?

Normally, this exercise has an almost instantaneous effect. The effect though depends on how deep you are in the trance state and how strong your will is. Another thing that has to be taken into consideration is your actual imbalance between masculine and feminine energies. If the imbalance is really acute you might not feel the effect right away. One of the sensations that marks the effect taking place in the bodies is your sexual energy calming down.

One of the pieces of logic behind the cross is that it can symbolize all masculine and feminine aspects: emotions and thoughts, magnetism and current, man and woman, Earth and sky and so on . . . If it is perfectly shaped it is balanced.

Why am I doing it?

To balance your inner polar energies.

In short

Balance the feminine and the masculine energies by visualizing an equal-armed cross and letting it influence and balance your energies.

Mental Body

In Western society we believe that if we understand something we have achieved a desirable state, transformation. Most of the information we encounter, regardless of how educational and informative it is, works on this mental level. At the root of it lies the idea of "understanding creates transformation." In the best-case scenario understanding removes obstacles and old beliefs (changing some energetic patterns on the mental level), but transformation requires action; actions make the transformation, actions lead to balance. So next time you see a nice educational and informative book, remember that it will create (at best) understanding, but not transformation, not change, without actions taken.

Thoughts are the other side of emotion and emotion is the other side of thoughts. They always come together, regardless of if you are able to experience every thought as emotion. Actually, most sensitive people can experience thoughts as emotions. Think of an apple: you have the thought of an apple, the previous experience of an apple and, if you move it aside, you can feel the ideal of "apple" in the shape of emotion. It is because we have ideas of things and astral copy of things. All things exist on many levels.

We can consider emotions and thoughts as two sides of a notion. They can be thought of as the same thing, but with different vibrations. Mind is high vibrations and emotion is low vibrations. Like poles of a magnet, thoughts are the positive, active, masculine energy of an idea while emotions are the negative, passive feminine. The positive energy is the shaping energy, the one that gives the shape, the design to the negative, passive energy. We like our thoughts and healthy reason to shape our world. Otherwise, we would just use the brain to justify emotional decisions. Thoughts are real and active energies and they live by the designation you give them. Thoughts design your world and life. Use them carefully.

For example, land is negative energy; you working on the land is positive. You are shaping the land. Matter is a negative energy (passive), vibration is positive (active). So emotion is negative (passive) and energy and thoughts are positive (active). Remember we said that consciousness interprets events by tagging the event in the subconsciousness register? This is an active, positive act, while the emotion here is the subject, passive, negative energy. The source of all balance is to balance positive and negative (or at least to not imbalance it so brutally). Like with the eyes, hands and brain hemispheres, too much emotions or too much mind is also an imbalance.

Of course we can consider thoughts and emotions as separate notions, and in some aspects they are separate and stand by themselves. But we do want to see them together and to see their relationship, as with consciousness and subconsciousness. We are trying to balance ourselves. By ourselves I mean the personality (or character); and by personality I mean the four bodies (or three in some traditions): physical, emotional, mental and etheric. Beyond the personality, we have to consider the emotions and the thoughts as separate.

The opposite goes for the consciousness and the subconsciousness. They are separate at the level of personality but have to be merged in higher levels of spiritual development (the subconsciousness is our previous programming while the consciousness is the present state of mind. If we don't feel present and making decisions in the present moment, the subconsciousness does it for us. Like driving an automatic car). Merged means that they have to work together as perfectly balanced tools. In short, for the sake of understanding at this level we look at the thoughts and the emotions as one scale with different vibrations. This is the level of the truth we want at the moment.

Thoughts occupy even more dimensions than the emotions (you are wherever your thoughts are). As we have seen, some dimensions are relevant only for the physical body but higher dimensions are for emotions, thoughts they influence down the physical body from higher vibrations to lower. This might sound weird to some people. You might say, "What is so amazing about the fact that I can go back in time in my mind, it does not mean I can time travel." In hypnosis or deep states of meditation you visit other dimensions, including your past, if you want. All actions taken there will have a direct effect on (make a change to) your current state.

Thoughts are real things and they are *active* if they are connected to or expressed with intention. They are strong when expressed with emotions. If you think or wish something to someone while you are angry you actively harm this someone. You as a sensitive will easily feel it, because for you, life is more than just physical appearance. If the thoughts are charged with high vibrations, which also means high rhythm, they travel and manifest much faster. Take a healer for instance; the higher their vibrations are the sooner the healing takes effect. There are different levels of healing. Some use etheric energy and some use mental.

Thoughts are real and they take place in higher realms, where they manifest faster—instantly in fact (it is the effect on the physical realm that is delayed). Regardless of the manifestation of the thought, thoughts are never erased from reality. Nothing you think ever disappears. Everything you think, especially using intention and emotion, lives and manifests.

Two things have to be in place before we can actively shape and control the energies of emotions by the power of thought: *awareness* and *concentration* (will, willpower or intention). The thing that develops the concentration does the same for the will, and the other way round.

Now when you know about those bodies (emotional and mental) we can complete the picture of the functional causes of illnesses. We have mentioned the connection between the ether and your health, so I feel like I owe you an explanation of the technical side, of the way it works and of the reasons.

When we have energy in a negative form (fear of something, for example), this energy exists in the subconscious and has a mental–emotional link. This energy acts like a magnet; it attracts the same energy from outside. Some healers can see this energy form, as "black" energy. This black energy gradually infiltrates your energetic bodies, starting from the subtle bodies and going in, until it reaches the specific organ that is connected to the fear (normally the kidneys or lungs). This energy moves the etheric body away from its proper place, disconnecting your spirit from the physical body, at the location of the fear. This organ does not receive energy and so develops an illness. Health is energetic movement at all levels in all channels. So it is good to begin healing from moving the energies and see what comes up.

It is very simple and mechanical: we are healthy as long as the inner state of our energies is clean and flows. When it is not, we attract this black energy that prevents the physical body from receiving vitality, the energies of life. The solution is also very simple and mechanical; take this negative magnetic energy out of the mental and emotional body and it will leave the physical one as well. Then you can apply whichever healing technique you prefer. We will learn how to do this in the subconsciousness cleansing.

The ordinary flow of energy in the body copies the mental, emotional and subconscious patterns. Those are your character, this is who you are. Who you are results in what kind of health you have. You can cure yourself by working on your character. This is a different level or plane compared to working via doctors or healers.

The same logic applies to lack of energy. When we are stressed or occupied by negative emotions we are too involved in what is going on and are experiencing a serious energetic deficiency. Our body cannot recover because the necessary energy is missing. Why do kids heal faster? Because they haven't wasted their energy yet. Long story short, health is energy.

Every alternative medicine works on the level of the energetic bodies, be it Reiki healing, herbs, Bach drops, acupuncture, or massage. These techniques all establish the energetic bodies and their proper functioning (remember that the subtle bodies influence the physical). But they are not always able to cleanse the reason, unfortunately.

One more thing: when working with and healing people, it is very easy to release them from negative energy. But this energy came into their bodies somehow and there is a reason for it. The reason is the person themself. After removing the negative energy, the person remains the same person, the same character, and they still carry the reason for the appearance of the negative energy. They will generate the same circumstances and bring more energy of the old kind (regardless of the healing). There is a lesson behind every illness, be it karmic or circumstantial. Make sure the person has learned the lesson before releasing the energies or healing. Otherwise, the karma will pass to the healer and the person will learn nothing.

Samskara and the energetic bodies

We accept one weird idea that our thoughts, emotions and physical impulses are automatic and predestined and we have very little ability to influence anything. Basically, we have all been taught to believe that those three bodies are a closed code. We know that some events can influence and even change us, and our belief states that it is a one-way change or "no coming back" situation. But if we change our belief regarding the no coming back into "yes coming back," we can undo the influence or the change.

The three bodies mentioned above (etheric, emotional and mental) in combination with the physical one construct whatever is called the lower self or the character (or personality). This holds every previous experience. Memories, traumas and every other similar energy that we have lived through. The energies kept in those bodies (the energetic history of our lives) have constant influence on our everyday lives and our decision-making. When we act upon them, we are observers but not actively participants in our lives.

Samskara (at least as I understand it) is the energetic imprint that we act upon. It is automatic action that comes as a result of the sum of all imprints. We are hostages of samskara, we are not free to decide; we are led by it and others use it against our will—if we lack willpower. If we had willpower and understanding we could choose how to act. But most people don't choose, they act upon samskara.

Samskara is active on the level of one of our above-mentioned bodies (some of it is active on all four levels at once). On the emotional level it is the nice and painful memories that influence our decision about which restaurant to pick, or which guy to date. Emotions are very strong magnets. Some people say we attract what we are afraid of; well, here is why. Samskara is the subconscious set of impulse, reflexes, beliefs and programing.

On the mental level it is our beliefs about money, about social norms, things we were told by our parents or other authorities (coach, teacher, rabbi, priest, yoga instructor, doctor and so on). All kinds of personal delusions that came from our own false conclusions. Actually, think for a second: everyone or any authority or entity that has power over you makes you believe in its power, or you accept it voluntarily, because of beliefs or fears (you are afraid, so you unwillingly allow them authority over you). Whoever has power over us has it only because we gave it to them by believing in some social order or other; and without will and reason we won't be able to get out of their control. People without will are easy to rule and are "good customers" (by which I mean easy to manipulate, convince or aggressively sell to).

Let us take it one step further: why do you believe that you need to take extra measures like pills or vaccines for illnesses like flu more than you believe that your immune system has the tools to kill the germs that cause them?

The physical origin of our body and its immune system is the same as that of germs—they are both from Planet Earth. They have been coexisting for long enough that the immune system knows them by sight and knows what to do about them. Beliefs cause imbalances that cause illness. We said earlier that energy flows in line with your thoughts. If you don't believe in your immune system, on some level (not on all of them) you aren't giving it energy.

The mental body has its masculine and feminine sides: consciousness and subconsciousness. It is not exactly that way; they are more like tools used in combination with the mental body. But for simplicity's sake, let us think of them as if they are parts of the mental body. Our mind is the matrix of beliefs and acceptances that the energetic flow goes through. Through this matrix everything in our life manifests. Consciousness holds the key to interpreting events before they are stored in the subconsciousness. But subconsciousness is the one that has the influence on our behavior.

If there is information in your mind that is approved by you (in other words, if you believe in it or accept it), it will influence your life. False beliefs like "my income depends on my boss" don't need to exist; don't create any ideas and thoughts, don't create wrong interpretations. No need to make these kinds of ties. You are the spirit, you are free, don't give yourself artificial ties. Don't create conditioning or stipulations. Be free. Some systems cultivate the belief that you are able to do more than you used to believe. This is so as to remove previous beliefs in your abilities, be it physical or otherwise.

On this level, no matter how much we think we are educated or civilized, we are simply glorified animals with false beliefs about enlightenment. On the chakra levels, most of us live on the level of *manipura* chakra, which is the animal level of consciousness, not human. We tend to think that everything—success, fortune—depends on us and our conscious actions and choices, but in fact it is our subconsciousness that plays the biggest part in our successes. At this stage your inner guides and intuition cannot reach your consciousness. But this is only up to the moment when you have the will and the motivation to change it. Then the tools will follow.

This stage is in power as long as you are on the level of running from pain or chasing pleasure, and at these stages you keep accumulating karma (regardless if it is good or bad karma). When you become a truth seeker (you feel the hunger for spirituality for the truth), when you realize that your soul (the level of your consciousness that is above the lower self) wants self-fulfillment you turn to the path of love and the universal guru comes to you in a certain form, be it a book, person or inner voice. We can turn to the way of spiritual seekers using our will and desire to serve others. *Running from pain* or *chasing pleasure* would turn into different levels of felicity. Pain would not be a threat and ordinary pleasure would not be a motivator. Then we can be released from karma (by the guru). If you don't see any other motivation but running from pain or chasing pleasure, that is absolutely fine. Do what is the most important for yourself as soul at the moment.

Samskara is an energetic formation caused by past events and it continually influences our lives. In other words, our past is influencing our lives, and from the point of view of emotions we always live in the past. Many of the decisions we make every minute—what to eat, where to go, with whom to meet—are made under this samskara. We don't belong to ourselves.

But as always, there are ways to change it. There is something stronger than samskara; it is called karma. Not the karma of previous lives (accumulation of actions), but the karma of the moment (THE action). The current moment is stronger than the past. Actually, the past exists in us in the form of samskara and the NOW is the eternal now. The eternal now is stronger than samskara. Karma (THE action) of the eternal now is stronger than samskara. Since we have both consciousness and subconsciousness, and our subconscious actions are our samskara and are not applicable to all new situations we encounter, in some situations we have to be conscious in the now so as not to act upon old samskara. Ask yourself now, where is my consciousness, where do I exist, am I present in my life?

We can make eternity an actual thing in our lives. If we want it to be on our side, we have to become one with it. After the meditation of eternity, the now is stronger than the samskara. And through combining what we have already looked at—our ability to reason and control the energies of our emotions by the power of thought—we get the perfect meditational exercise to equip us with the tools we need to balance the mental body (the mind).

Two things have to be in place before actively shaping and controlling the energies of emotions by the power of the thought: *awareness* and *concentration* (will, willpower or intention). Whatever develops the ability of concentration does the same to the will, and the other way round. Both are developed by the exercise below.

∞ main exercise ∞
Meditation (or relaxation) of eternity

Meditation is a valuable tool for many problems and at the same time a super-booster of spiritual development. There are a tremendous number of books about the benefits of meditation, easily found. So this mission, of explaining about the benefits of meditation, really falls on someone else's shoulders. But it is still important for me to emphasize the points that follow.

We have two kinds of thought: flowing thought and aware thought. Flowing thought is a chain of thoughts our brain generates without our active participation. Normally, the chain is made up of links made by association. You see something, it reminds you of something else, that reminds you of a totally unrelated thing but in your mind it is linked somehow, and so on without end. The flowing mind can get stuck on an idea or a problem to be solved and start to generate "solutions" and see their weak points. It can be harmless or harmful—for example if it is at the expense of sleep.

The other kind of thought is aware thought, the kind that is generated by your own will, for example when we analyze, or try to be creative. The difference is that the first kind of thought does not have a center, while the second has. It is the same with meditation; in meditation your thoughts (mind activity) have a center that you define. For this specific meditation, the center is the notion of eternity.

Both meditation and relaxation have the same purpose and technique; the principle is: what you think, you become. In both you have the effort of the conscious mind that undertakes the job. In other words, the word "relaxation" does not reflect the relaxation of the mind, but the body only. The main differences are in posture (in meditation we sit and in relaxation lie down) and the position of the hands (in meditation we make *mudras*, in relaxation we have the hands palms up). Another difference is that in meditation it is harder to fall asleep, while in relaxation it is very easy, especially if you do it while you are tired, at sunset or close to bedtime. From here on, most of the points made relate to both meditation and relaxation.

Meditation builds willpower by the act of will we use every time our mind leaves the center and switches to flowing thoughts, which is the idea around which we meditate. The efforts we put in to bring our mind back to the center are called will or willpower. By doing so we build this muscle called willpower, will, concentration or intention. All are one.

Meditation creates awareness. When we manage not to let our mind switch to flowing thoughts and stay concentrated on the center of the meditation, we widen our awareness, the presence of us, of the active us (or the truth self?) in the moment (or the center of the meditation). In simple terms, we gain awareness regarding the center of the meditation.

The center of our meditation is eternity, and eternity is one of the business cards of the central universal mind (and beyond) that is called God. By meditating on eternity we do not just align with the eternal now but also synchronize with God vibrations of eternity, with the Godly side of us.

Another thing about meditation: God has constant connection with every particle that exists and of course with me and you. There is no force in the universe that can break this connection. Our connection, the one between me and God is unique. In this connection the only participants are God and me. There is no one near, in between, and no mediators. Only God and I have eternal quality time with each other. God's attention is always on me, while my attention is rarely on God. Our attention is everywhere: on flowing thoughts, on things that draw our attention, on things we find interesting, on obsessive thoughts and whatnot. But while meditating we turn our attention to God, and we strengthen the connection between God and us (in fact "strengthening" is not really correct; we strengthen our ability to realize this connection). This connection is not something we have to earn or deserve; we have it by default and no one, nothing, not even us ourselves, can break it for good. Just to clarify, we turn our attention to God when we hold the idea of God as a focus in our meditation. When we direct our attention to God and stay that way. In meditation on eternity, only one of the characteristics of God is the center of the meditation—eternity.

———

Later on I will introduce full instructions for how to meditate, but before that I must give you a choice. There are two ways to learn meditation: inner and outer. The outer is the full instructions that follow later. The inner is the intriguing one.

In the inner method (otherwise known as open meditation), in which you normally don't have a fixed center (at least at the beginning), all you need to know about meditation is that you must not follow your flowing thoughts, and every time you catch yourself flowing with the mind you must bring your mind back to the beginning—the state of zero doing or zero acting.

You do not need to think or know anything about posture, hand position, back, breathing: nothing. You just sit and say: "I am meditating now." Every time you catch your mind drifting away, you say: "Hey, I am meditating now." Everything else will come by observation, intuition and awareness. No one is teaching you, you learn by pure individual experience, eventually discovering your personal meditation.

There are pros and cons. The inner method is suitable for people who are on the spiritual development path or at least have this attitude. It takes more time to get into actual meditating (around twenty days). It is not for everyone and requires the character and the will to do it. In other words, it is for real enthusiasts. So if this inner method of open meditation speaks to you and attracts you, stick with it; you can always come back and read the other meditation instructions later.

Just remember that we do have a center and the center is eternity, the notion, the idea and most importantly the feeling. Every time you catch your mind running away from the feeling of eternity, you tell it: "Hey, eternity." If you feel like it, you can start meditating even without this center of eternity and start using this center later . . .

Time and duration
Once a day, for a minimum of 20 minutes (40 days in a row).

What to do (for relaxation)
Lie down, relax, set your feelings on the notion of eternity and enjoy the feeling.

How to do it (for relaxation)
Lie on the back, hands at the sides with the palms towards the sky (savasana). Breathe deeply and slowly. Prepare for total relaxation. Visualize the pole of light, the one from the exercise, for protection.

Imagine a spiritual teacher or yoga instructor is telling you to relax, breathe slowly, direct the attention inside, relax the head, brain, spine, eyes, tongue, neck, throat, until the whole head is relaxed. Keep relaxing gradually from the neck down to the lower back and do the same at the front of the body. Imagine your spiritual teacher is naming your body parts one by one, from top to bottom. Every part the teacher names, you relax. You can do this by relaxing the whole body, either from the crown of the head to the toes or from the toes to the head.

Alternatively, just imagine one ray of gold as wide as your shoulders coming from the sky, going down from your head to your toes; every part of the body it touches relaxes. The ray can also come from the toes up.

Release yourself from all limitations by concentrating on what makes you limitless, what gives you absolute freedom. When you have no feeling of your body and are completely relaxed, free yourself from the surroundings. Imagine that you are in an open space or flying in the skies. You are free from your body and your surroundings.

Now think of the universe, of its infinity and its eternity. What feeling does the notion of eternity awake in you? If you can't find the feeling this way, just repeat the word "eternity." Concentrate on this feeling, let it grow, let it take over every part and every cell of your body, be attuned to it and live it, be it. When the feeling is vivid enough, tell yourself: "I am part of eternity." How does it make you feel? Live this feeling. Let the vibrations of the feeling become part of you, of your physical body, your inner organs, your head. You can let this vibration into your spine and into the head. It can be overwhelming; if you feel this, just try pinching yourself, or start breathing consciously.

After twenty minutes of experiencing the feelings of eternity and "I am part of eternity" (and the calmness it brings), tell yourself that it is time to get back to reality. It is very important to be gradual in how you return your consciousness from the state of meditation to the physical reality. Shift your attention from the feelings to the breathing; realize the body, every part of it. The room and the surroundings, your position in the room. The touch of your clothes and the feeling of the air on the skin. Rub your palms together to warm them. Place them on the eyes, creating a layer of protection, and open the eyes into the darkness. Smile; remember the good feelings. Keep these feelings throughout the day. You can turn and lie on your right or left side for a few moments. Once you are seated, you can rub your palms together again and place them on another part of the body, wherever you feel like; and again on a third part. Do not try to do it more than three times; the energetic flow from the hands will be fully absorbed after three parts.

Remember to turn off the pole of light.

Do this for 40 days, for a minimum 20 minutes of actual engagement with the feeling of eternity (25–30 minutes total). The best time, for the majority of people, is the morning, as this is the time when we have energetic inflow. The most difficult times to meditate are generally around noon and later in the day, especially at sunset.

What to do (for meditation)

Sit in a comfortable position, tongue folded upwards, relax, set your feelings on eternity and enjoy the feeling.

How to do it (for meditation)

Sit in a comfortable position and keep your back (especially the lower back) straight. Your sitting position is very important to the exercise, especially having a straight back. If at the beginning of the exercise we are not sitting comfortably, the discomfort will prevent us from disconnecting from the body. Have some props to sit on, like pillows, folded towels or books. When you sit, straighten your back and relax. If you are not comfortable, reduce or add more props until you can sit with a straight back and relax your body.

Fold your tongue back from the middle. This creates a link that connects the upper and lower "dental bridges" of the mouth; the gums behind the front teeth, upper and lower. The fingers are intertwined and the hands rest in the lap.

Put on protections. Do the gradual relaxation exercise from the top down or down to the top of your body, as in the relaxation.

You have to be relaxed to the point of not feeling your physical body and not sensing your surroundings. Try to visualize yourself somewhere that encourages this criterion. It could be a swimming pool; you could be floating in the air, in outer space or anything you like. Release yourself from limitations, remember what makes you limitless.

From here on, it is the same as with the relaxation. Set the mind on eternity, concentrate on the feeling it brings, feel how it is to be a part of eternity (because you actually are). After twenty minutes, gradually return to reality. When you are back, rub the palms together and place them over the eyes, then open the eyes into the protected dark space the palms create. Try to keep the feeling with you throughout the day.

Turn off the pole of light.

What not to do
- When in your sitting position, don't lean or otherwise support the back or the head. If it is difficult to keep the back straight, you can sit on books, cushions, a folded towel or yoga bricks. Use as much height as you need for the back to be straight. When you find the right height, you will be able to sit upright almost effortlessly. If you need to, though, you can sit in an upright chair.
- It is very important to put in protections; use the pole of light for this purpose.
- Some people use music to enter the meditative state or to relax; but don't do this.

How and when do I know it's working?
It is normal if at the beginning you don't feel eternity, or the thoughts of space does not bring the eternity feeling. You can think of anything you believe is eternal: God, energy, or anything else. The feeling will

come, and will disappear and will come again. It is also okay if your body's discomfort does not let you get into a meditative state. Keep exercising. Soon your body will find a place of comfort and you will be able to disconnect your mind from it.

When you feel eternity and the meaning of it and the vibrations of eternity become part of your system, you will know you are on the right path. Just keep going. There is no such thing as meditation not working. It is our ability to feel the process that has to be developed—and will be developed if we keep working at it.

Why am I doing it?

This meditation/relaxation is intended to introduce you to the actual reality of the eternal now and its power over samskara and your previous experiences. To disconnect from previous experiences, to build awareness and willpower and to become one with God in his eternal sense, to resonate with God. To realize that the only limitations that exist, exist only because you believe in them. Everything is limitless, absolutely everything. God is limitless and God is everything and everything is God.

An additional tremendous benefit is accumulation of psychic energy. When we use our brain (or it uses itself in the action of flowing mind) we burn some of this psychic energy. If our brain or the mouth, or both, cannot shut up all day, we burn it all. While meditating the brain is silent (as is the mouth) and the stream of the psychic energy accumulates. Why is this important? Your intuition, super-consciousness, connection with higher self, inner balance and more magical things that we can develop all operate using this level of energy.

In short

With 20 minutes of exercise, you can give yourself the feeling of eternity and of being part of it, and keep this feeling for the rest of the day.

◦ᷝ complementary exercise ᷝ◦
Quieting the mind

Western civilization doesn't let the mind rest; we always "need" to be connected, to consume more information and to satisfy our empty curiosities. Everything attracts and demands our attention, thus our energy. We waste tremendous amounts of energy. At some point it becomes second nature (if not first) and something that we justify; we believe it is necessary and right to be connected, to know what is going on with our friends, in the world, on the stock market. To read more articles for the sake of knowing stuff, so we can show off with useless "interesting facts" we heard the other day on some animal documentary.

The left side of the brain was not designed to take over all elements of our lives, let alone be raised to the position of the rightful king of our society to whom we own our technological advances. Scholars of the European Renaissance believed that people can find happiness using their minds. That happiness depends on us and it is within our ability to create our happiness, since only we know what is happiness for us. The people of the Renaissance were looking for alternative sources to the holy writings.

The idea that only we know what makes us happy is fundamental. As we will see later in the book, the mind is not the part that knows; the mind is not the leader but the servant. The mind cannot generate inspiration or believe in universal values or love someone, or even love itself. I am skipping forward a bit but I will tell you that the heart knows all those answers and the heart is the one that can experience love, inspiration and happiness; and it knows what can make us happy. Not the physical but the energetic equivalents or doubles of the heart: etheric and emotional.

This idea, that we know what makes us happy, has become the sales slogan for every commercial. This idea is used by capitalism and blown out of proportion. It has given birth to romantic consumerism, the mind shrunk to the left side of the brain and happiness to short-lived pleasures.

As a result, we are imbalanced, left-brain-sided creatures who are ruled by these implanted wishes and disconnected from our own (real) desires.

Spoiler alert: we are not created to consume but to create. Only creation from the heart, with joy and enthusiasm, will bring us real satisfaction; when we do what we are meant to do, we feel joy in doing it.

⸺

But first let us silence the brain. The left side of the brain, overloaded as a result of misuse or work, or for any other reason, does not stop until you have exhausted all your energies. Some people cannot fall naturally asleep at night after a day at work. They have to play online games or watch TV to get to sleep. Others, in order to silence the left side of the brain, drink alcohol or smoke weed, all acts that burn the psychic energy and put them into an energetically vulnerable state.

I don't need to tell you how bad all those solutions are for sensitives (and for others as well). If you exhaust all your psychic energy, there can be no spiritual growth and no creativity. Drinking and smoking activates alpha brain waves and burns psychic energy, leaving you in an opened state, unprotected.

So here are some easy, fast and effective tricks to put the left side of the brain to rest. Hopefully, if you follow the book's exercises and meditations, your mind will be under your control, and most of the time silent, like it is supposed to be.

If you have been following the instructions so far and doing the main exercises (not to mention the complementary ones), reading these lines should have reminded you about yourself before you started working on the balance. It will have shown you the difference between you then and now. Shown you that we don't need anything from outside (apart from guidance) to be balanced and happy. Everything we need we have inside. We don't need pills, alcohol, weed, music, the outer world or anything else.

Some tricks to quiet the mind

While the left side of the brain is working like crazy, it sucks the energies from the whole body, shrinking the energetic centers and leaving the body dry of energy. Every time we demand better performance from our brain we enlarge the energetic center in the head so it can deliver. As a result, all the chakras of the body except the head one are small and empty. Later we will introduce an exercise that balances the chakras. But here is what to do for now. Don't forget to use intention while doing the exercise.

Think of the mathematical figure zero. See the shape of it in your mind and what it represents: nothing, zero activity, zero moving, zero creating. Let this zero occupy your mind and transfer the idea of nothing, of no action and those vibrations onto your bodies in the area around your head. Feel how the vibration of zero is absorbed by the energetic fields around you and your head.

Imagine the energetic field generated by the disproportionate work of the brain around your head, and see how a wire of copper connects the field with the center of Earth. How all the generated energy around the head goes via the wire to the center of the planet. It releases you from the unwanted overload.

Now, using your intention, shrink the energetic center to a normal size (around ping-pong ball size); meanwhile enlarge the heart chakra to the same size and see how the energetic potential between the two centers is balanced.

Take an imaginary blackboard sponge and erase the information around your head and in it, as if the information was chalk writings on the blackboard. Now keep erasing the information around the whole energetic field around the body.

Switch your attention to the heart (the energetic heart); feel its calmness and special vibe. Breathe deeply and slowly. Inhale, hold and, as slowly as possible, exhale. Do it a few times until you feel complete calmness. Don't let the brain take over; keep your attention on the breathing or the heart. When a nice feeling appears, turn your attention to it. It means that you have withdrawn yourself from the left side of the brain and the alpha waves of the brain have been activated.

All these steps work perfectly as individual acts and even better as a chain of actions. Another trick that can be used is yogic *mudras,* which are really intended for reaching higher states of mind but which for us can be used to turn off or silence the brain and thus calm down your mind.

If you have been delegating more responsibilities to your left hand, by now the left side of your brain will be less "aggressive" in the sense of being the commander of our life over which we have no control.

In any case, you can always initiate some activity with your left hand while the right is resting quietly. This will gradually turn your left side off and awaken the right side of your brain.

Just to add another thing, there are some links or reflexes related to our brain habits, when you do one thing and it provokes the other. For example, if you work on a PC, and your work is related to the left side of the brain, every time you look at a PC screen you "tense" the left side of the brain to do your job and you narrow your vision. By doing so, you create a reflex; your body remembers that when you look at the screen you work with the left side of your brain. Now every time you look at a screen or narrow your vision for reasons unrelated to your work, your brain's left side will be activated. Observe your behavior and when you find those reflexes try not to act on them.

Shambhavi and akashi mudras

The original purpose of these exercises is to awake the super-consciousness, but it is also a good way to let the mind rest or support a meditative state of mind (trance). It is traditionally performed in the lotus posture but can easily be done in any sitting posture you prefer, even sitting on your beloved sofa.

Shambhavi mudra is performed by looking at the point between the eyebrows. Yes, it is impossible to see this point, but we keep looking. With the eyes open, we direct our attention to the point between the eyebrows but all we see is two bows and a "V" between them. If you can, or with time, you will be able to close the eyes. In some traditions the head has to be leaned back around 30–45 degrees. Before performing the *mudra* three times, take a deep breath and exhale very slowly.

Akashi mudra is performed by sitting straight while leaning the head back 90 degrees, eyes looking up or in *shambhavi mudra*. You bend the head back on an inhale and return it on an exhale. It all sounds so yogic but is really very simple. When your neck is relaxed and the head bent back (you can add to this looking to the point between the eyebrows, or just up) you will feel like you want to go to sleep, or as if you are going into alpha brain waves (trance or meditation mode). In this state it is very difficult for the left side of the brain to perform hard work. Do the same here, first breathing deeply three times and then performing the *mudra*. When you exhale, do it very slowly.

Controlling the rhythm

When we control the rhythm we control the mind, otherwise the mind controls the rhythm. It is very much true for controlling the breathing. But also pay attention to the rhythm of your actions and how your brain jumps to the next task before finishing with the current. See how you move, type, walk, eat, drink and speak—observe your behavior and rhythm. The rush of your brain affects all the actions of the body; it translates as stress and changes the body's natural rhythm.

Rather than just believe those ideas and go along with the brain, letting it dictate the rhythm, we need to be more in control of what we think of as urgent, to see the bigger picture. I would suggest you pay close attention to your actions and to the rhythm with which they are performed. Every time you catch yourself rushing, stop, slow down, and keep working with just a slightly slower rhythm. Don't let people around you suck you into their rush. Live your own rhythm.

A very good solution is the control of your breathing. You control your body's breathing, you control it all. It is not a coincidence that in yoga and martial arts breathing is placed at the base and in the center of the practices. The calmness of the mind is achieved by the calmness of the *prana*, and the calmness of the *prana* is achieved by calm and rhythmic breathing.

Regardless of if you breathe from the chest or the belly or even perform full yogic breathing, control the rhythm of your breath. Concentrate on your breathing and make it rhythmically even: inhale equals exhale. The longer they are the calmer you will get. Start with a minimum of three seconds (three in, three out). It is very good to practice breathing twice a day till you make rhythmic breathing part of your life, but it is even useful to do it ad hoc. When you notice that you are in a rush, stop and start breathing rhythmically. Find a calm rhythm and let it influence the body and the rhythm of your actions.

If you want to have even more control of the rhythm, learn to breathe rhythmically based on your heartbeat. Start with three beats: inhale for three beats and exhale for three beats. Do it twice a day and with time you will be able to move up to four and four.

This is one of the best favors you can do yourself; it will align you with the rhythm of the universe. Your calm, natural heartbeat is aligned with the universe and by breathing in that rhythm you will be as well.

—

I would warmly recommend that you implement full yogic breathing as part of your life. This kind of breathing charges the whole body with energy *(prana)*, helps the ventilation of the entire volume of the lungs and helps the *anahata* chakra to receive *prana*. I am singling out this chakra because the heart receives energy from there; and we already know that when the head is in a rush, it sucks the energy like crazy, and this energy comes from the lower parts, mainly the heart.

Some of the symptoms of a weak *anahata* chakra (heart energetic center) are: insomnia, overthinking and mind restlessness, depression, hopelessness, and lack of enthusiasm, determination and willpower. You can find many good examples of how to develop the habit of full yogic breathing online and in books on the subject.

What not to do
Don't go back to old habits of disturbing your natural rhythm.

How and when do I know it's working?
When you feel like you are about to rush but something pops up in you and you think for a split-second and do things with the new rhythm. This means that the new habits you have been developing are starting to become a part of you.

Why am I doing it?
To quiet the mind and obtain control over the rhythm of your life.

In short

Tell the mind shhhhhh, through use of *mudras*, controlled breathing and awareness of the chakras.

Note: There are many other exercises to develop and master the mind, but they are not advisable, in my opinion, while you are not in balance.

4

Principles of Exercise

I am glad and excited for you that you have reached this stage of the book. It means you have been working on yourself and are achieving some progress (and you have survived my writing). You also have accumulated some mistakes along the way, and some questions. This is the point for us to look at the principles of the exercises.

I say principles of the *exercises* but it is much broader than this. It is the principles of energetic work. Since everything is energy, with time you will see how those principles apply to many other spheres of life.

The reason we are looking at the principles of the exercises now is that to appreciate them you have to have worked on the exercises, felt them, seen how it is to be an active part of the energetic realm and what are the laws and effects of this realm. So let's begin.

KISS—Keep It Simple, Stupid

I have put much thought into the description of each exercise. The description is exactly what you have to read and to do, not more and not less. Of course in some places I have said more regarding the effects or the feelings of the exercise, but I've never given extra information on the practical side of the performance of the exercise.

This is the energetic realm we are dealing with, the one you are sensing with your sensitivity. This realm has its own laws and effects. Apart from sensing it to the level of becoming overwhelmed, we don't know much of it. One of the goals of the exercises is to become gradually familiar with this realm.

At this point, reflect on your practice of the exercises so far. It is very common for us to imagine, adjust or change things as we work through them. So go back to the descriptions of the exercises you are working on here. Read them again and compare them with the actual way you have been doing it. Work on doing them as described.

Every Practice Must Become Permanent

Our goal is to make the effect of every exercise permanent or at least long-lasting. This is achieved by regular practice of the exercise, by regular use of the "muscles" that this exercise is building and by doing the exercise in trance. It is very similar to when we learn something and then our body can do it without our participation, like driving, swimming or walking.

I will explain about trance later. As for the regular exercise and the "muscles," while performing a certain exercise, we change our original state into a desirable state.

When we work with the candle, for example, we build an inner balance and strengthen the inner concentration. If we work for long enough, the effect will become part of us permanently; we will feel it not only during the exercise but for the entire day. This is obviously different for every individual, and also depends on exactly how and how much we do the exercises.

If later we use those "muscles" for other things, like protection, healing, energetic cleansings or other psychic activity, we won't need to exercise any more. The effect will stay for as long as we use them.

This is why we have to meditate for forty days in a row. This is the time needed for the subject of your meditation, the center, to become part of your energetic system. But it applies only to meditations that have the purpose of "installing" new vibrations. Like eternity, in our case. In order to "uninstall" the new state, the new vibrations, you have to go back to the previous state and "meditate" on it, or be exposed to its negative effect, for quite a while.

By the way, at some point the exercise will become instant. After working on the candle for some time, you will sit in front of it one day, preparing to visualize, and you will discover that just as you think to visualize the candle will appear in your mind, effortlessly, just like that. The same with the energetic balls; at some point the balls will move themselves and you will just watch. This is the stage at which you know that the energetic channel is there and stable.

The Principle of Resonance

This principle says that we are compatible (resonate) with some people on some topics and not on others, while we are incompatible with other people in other ways. With some friends we have a good time while cooking; with others we like studying together.

But we often have friends and people around us whose presence "eliminates" our creative flow. These people are still part of our lives and we do not want it to stop being so, but it is important to be aware when our energies are incompatible or in dissonance.

The same applies to energetic practices and exercises. When you have good resonance with your partner, friend or spiritual guide, the process of your actions is boosted greatly. This is one of the ways in which we consciously pick a guru (although in fact, when our time comes and we are ready, the universe will pick and show us our teacher). But if you feel that your spiritual advisor, or yoga instructor, everyone likes is not resonating with you, maybe you should consider finding the one who does resonate with you. By the way, the principle of resonance is also we pick our sexual partners.

You can find a place and a friend or partner to do the exercises with. Resonance is not the sum of your energies, it is the multiplicity of them. Work with people who you have resonance with, work in groups; the more people the better. The resonance elevates your potential, making the effect faster and longer-lasting. When you get to the peak of your potential, regardless of the field of work, a person who has good resonance with you will push your potential forward.

Resonance works as long as the energetic potential between you has not fulfilled itself. This brings us to the next principle:

Potential Cycles of Energies

Why do some things excite us only for a certain amount of time? Why do we have great sex with some partners only a limited number of times? Why is something interesting only for a while and some of the exercises stop working after a while?

The answer is energetic potential. When you work on something you work with the energetic level of the thing that you are able to access. It becomes a part of you and you create something in the universe using its energies. When the energetic flow ends, this is a sign that the potential has been exhausted. We have spoken about rhythm; this is it.

I will try to illustrate using the example of a few exercises. The candle exercise: let's imagine it has taken you a while to start feeling the effect of the candle. The effect has been coming and going but with time has become stronger. One day you feel the effect like never before. The exercise is successful, the effect is deep and long-lasting. It has even left a good feeling, a reward of a sort, and you feel very proud of your accomplishment. The next day, you sit to do the candle remembering yesterday's success. You do absolutely the same steps as yesterday, but the effect is not as strong as it was then. There are just some weak sparks of success here and there. Some of us might concentrate on the good feeling that comes with the *memories* instead of actually doing the exercise. The next day, you might feel nothing despite the glory of the success of two days ago.

Why is that and what to do? I am not going to tell you . . . Joking! If you have ever practiced something for a while, anything that requires you to learn more and get better, you know how those days of peaks happen here and there, and that after them an emptiness naturally appears. If you are an artist, you know that when you create, you build something and this something is built inside you, simultaneously. When this something is ready, you feel sudden emptiness. We spoke of three periods of life and about how after the fulfillment of the energy called karma, we feel emptiness.

Developing good and bad habits work on the same principle. People who want more money, power, safety or whatever, from the point of acquiring their latest fulfillment, will feel empty after a while.

This is the law of evolution. The entity we call God, the ultimate God, is always new. The energies never repeat themselves. We are neurons in God's system, neurons with the potential to become gods. We act in the system in accordance with God's nature, which we call laws of the universe. In other words, we are subject to these laws and we are on the path of evolution (consciously or not, but consciously is better; this is a part of the spiritual path). In combination with the law of rhythm, we move from energetic potential to energetic lack of potential and then back to energetic potential but on a new scale. Only at a certain level of consciousness and spiritual development can one be introduced to higher principles where we can overcome the law of rhythm. (Intriguing, no? To always have universal energies that are at your disposal without having to be subject to the law of rhythm.)

Long story short, every energy has its charge, like a battery. When the charge is spent, we have emptiness. Understanding this principle is very important for life. Look for the emptiness, don't try to relive the past. Go to the next potential, but do it with new tools. You cannot reach new peaks that are more exciting than the previous ones with the same tools with which you reached the previous peak.

How does this translate to the practical side of the exercise? When you feel the peak, wait for the emptiness, look for new ways to do the exercise, be patient and trust your intuition. After the peak, have the attitude of a beginner; forget about previous successes—they are now part of you but they are irrelevant for the future peaks.

With the balance, for example, at the beginning it seems like the balance is reached very fast. But as we go forward, we have new aspects to balance. So if you feel like you have reached the balance but after a while you get to feel that something is not in place, it is not because you are going back, but because you are going forward. Only when you stop working on yourself for a long time will you start going back. It is the law of nature: whatever doesn't move forward, slides back. Balancing does not end here. After balancing ourselves on the current level, we will have the opportunity to balance the next level, and so on.

It is the same with meditation; you found a way to evoke the feeling of eternity, at some point it was strong, and you kept the feeling with you for the whole day. But on the next day, you use the same way to evoke the feeling but it is not there any more. Trying harder to squeeze the old way for more feelings of eternity won't work; find new ways. Become a beginner again. And this brings us to the next principle.

Zero Expectations and Fresh Beginnings

Short and catchy!

Every time you are about to perform an exercise, have the attitude of a baby exploring the world. Babies, when encountering the new, don't have expectations, they don't have opinions or previous experience, they are not corrupted, they are always new, always fresh and always look for new things to explore. Later we will look at inner baby meditation.

Before beginning the exercise or meditation, forget about the past, the feelings and the methods you were using. Start fresh, from a blank page. Why is this important? When you work on the exercises you engage your creative abilities, you create new realities within yourself. As we have said before, thoughts are real. When you sit to meditate and feel like the current meditation is the continuation of the previous, you have got to the place that you created before. Here, there is no energetic potential, only your previous thoughts and experience. Here, there is no emptiness. And you find yourself "meditating" in the past, in your own thoughts of the past. It is not so obvious at the beginning, but will be later, when you understand the energetic world and your sensitivity helps you see things.

The Principle of Attention

What happens when we meditate? We focus our *attention* on something (the center of the meditation) and bring the *attention* back to the center every time it runs away. With time, the center of the meditation grows stronger, we accumulate willpower and psychic energy. So our *attention* is the natural flow of energy. Like an opened tap, the water always flows and it is up to us where to direct it.

Most of us waste this energy, mainly on nothing that is really important. We are weak, we don't have willpower, we don't know what we want and we run after pleasures, easy gratification, or fake rewards. We are left-brain-hemisphere people and we don't belong to ourselves. If we are sensitive, we are doomed. Apart from us being wasteful on behalf of this magical energy, we are being manipulated into giving it to others, the ones around us, and the ones on the other side of our phone screen, all fighting for your attention.

While meditating or doing other kinds of exercises, focus your attention on a point. I mention in every exercise where to put the attention. When the attention runs away, gently bring it back to the point of work. The spot your attention is on is the spot of the actual work. No attention, no work. While not engaged in meditations, esoteric or energetic practices, it is best to keep your attention inside yourself.

In many cases, doing the exercises gives us a nice feeling. In some cases, like the meditation on eternity, we have to keep our attention on the center of the meditation or exercise, not on how it makes us feel. How it makes us feel is just is a kind of pleasant distraction. In the candle or other exercises that involve the states of trance, a nice feeling comes up. And what do we do? We switch to the nice feeling, forget about the exercise, give me more of the nice feeling. And then the exercise is over, because your attention is not on the subject of the exercise but on the feeling.

On the same principle, we feed what we think of. If the left side of our brain is stuck on negativity and we cooperate, we feed the negativity. If we fight against something or with something we feed it. Yes, we do. We just feed the other side with a different kind of attention, but we still feed it. Giving too much attention to a problem won't solve it.

There is another principle that is very much the continuation of this one. When we meditate or do other exercises, we "install" new vibrations instead of the old ones. This can be illustrated with the example of mining. The rock is the old energies and the empty space is the new ones, but we want to concentrate here on the broken stones that are left, the rock we removed to build the cave or the tunnel. Or, to be exact, we don't want to be concentrated on them. **Never concentrate on what is leaving your body.** By feeding something outside we feed it inside. By paying attention to the energy leaving, we are kind of returning it.

When I introduce energetic cleansings, all this will be clearer. Because when we cleanse ourselves energetically, we remove the energy we don't want, and it is very interesting to have a look at those energies we remove.

A good way to help our body to get rid of the old vibrations is sport or other exercise. I particularly advise yoga, because it engages every part of the body and helps to cleanse the energies using breathing, posture and relaxation. Other kinds of activity do not reach this level of engagement and depth of cleansing.

Now, think for a second about how you fight with bad habits, and how by fighting them you feed them from the back door. The solution to this is to concentrate on the thing that has to come instead of the bad habit. If you sleep late, for example, imagine what you do when you get up early, and how it feels. If you smoke, imagine that at the times you usually smoke each cigarette you hug your kids instead, or smile at the sun, or read a book you like, or anything else. Even if it is not going to become your new habit, it doesn't matter as long as you have switched your attention from the act of fighting to the solution or something else. It is the same in spiritual development: we switch from who we don't want to be into who we want to be. And this new *who we want to be* becomes our new subject, new future, new inspiration, so reallocating the energetic resources from negative paths to positive. From what I don't want, into what I want.

Energy, attention for bad habits is like oxygen; so leave them no energy. Like a path in the woods—when people stop using it, grass grows all over it until you cannot see it any more. Habits are like this path: if we stop walking on them and instead give our attention to new paths, the old ones will disappear. What else works this way? The connections between neurons and all our repetitive actions, which turn into habits. These are energetic channels, and the energy is like an open tap and your willpower is the regulator of the directions.

Exercise while in trance

Soon we will speak more about the trance state of mind (I also call it the meditative or alpha state) and how it is relevant to balancing for sensitives. The alpha state (or, as I like to call it, the alpha realm) is the space in which your subconsciousness exists; we have looked at the subconsciousness already.

Many of the exercises are done while we are in this state, because then the imprint of our work is stronger and faster. Energetic cleansings are also done in this state. This is a state in which we are vulnerable and we have to cleanse and protect it; but more about this later. It is very important not to forget to leave this state after finishing the exercise or meditation, since it is a very vulnerable state. I will elaborate on this later.

By this point, you know how this stage feels, how to get there and out of there. Later, when you are balanced, stable and your energetic potential is strong, you will be able to stay in this state all the time.

When we work with energies we tend to use our own energy. However, this is not the right way, regardless of if we are doing exercises, cleansing energies or healing people. We should be just the tool or the channel, never the battery. Energetic management is very important. Our energy has to be clean of other people's energies and we must have enough of it that we do not feel the lack of it. We need to have more energy every day (we tend to have less and less energy every day, sadly). So when you exercise **use the *prana* around you,** not your own energy.

When we create energetic balls, we use *prana;* when we have to visualize, we use *prana*. When we feel very generous and we want someone else to feel good, we don't give them our energy (it is actually harmful) but instead become a channel for universal energy. In cleansings and in protection we use the energy around us. If you feel that when you create protection or make energetic balls or anything else it exhausts you, this means you are using your own energy. In this case, before doing anything concentrate on the *prana* and let this energy serve your needs instead.

Note: In general, if you are not a healer, please refrain from applying anything to other people.

Emotions enlarge the effect of the exercise

This is a great illustration of how emotions bring energetic flow with them. The scale of the emotion is the amount of energy it brings. Normally, we are "programmed" to use this energy for the emotion itself (for example, when we feel sad we concentrate on sadness). But why? If you are angry, you burn the energy on the emotion of anger (it gets you nowhere); when you are excited you jump or dance or sit with a smile like a crazy person. It seems like only while we are afraid we use the energy in the "proper" way—to fight or escape.

Let us abstract for a moment from the natural link between the emotion and the action we take when feeling it. We have emotions and we have their triggers; we also know it is unhealthy to suppress emotions. What is left for us is, in energetic exercises and any other related activity, to harness those energies to use them for our purposes.

So, we can use the energies that stand behind emotions to do things. For now, concentrate on doing exercises while under the influence of some emotion. Think of joy, happiness or love. When you feel the stream of the energy from the emotion (that is, when you are experiencing the emotion), hold it and perform the exercise.

Different exercises have different effects. Some awaken energy, others balance it. In some cases, we have a lot of creative energy but don't have the necessary inspiration to use it, or know where to aim those energies. Sometimes we have more masculine energies, other times more feminine. When the imbalance is small and short, it is not a problem. But if it has not been balanced for a long time, it can lead us to unhealthy places.

Up to this point, the exercises I describe here are all balanced and protect and promote balance, but later we will look at some exercises that are very strong and bring energy that has to be balanced, for example the early awakening of the *kundalini*. In these kinds of exercises, if you are not ready, they will bring all the dirty energies to your consciousness, all your fears, and symptoms of illnesses. I will also give you counter-exercises to balance and protect yourself.

With time, you will intuitively feel when you want to do an exercise and which one, or which exercise balances other ones out, and so on.

The energetic characteristic to which we refer most of the time is vibration. This is to say energetic quality, its information and purpose. Every piece of energy has characteristics, or vibrations. Our body has vibrations; when we express or experience something we receive or send energy and that energy has vibration. It is the most basic yet the broadest adjective we use when we speak of energies. We can say either energies or vibrations but we really mean the same thing.

During an average day, we pay attention to our body only when something pleasant or unpleasant happens. In other words, when energy enters the body or leaves the body. The same goes for the quality of the energy, or vibrations. We feel them only when they come or when they go. If we meditate on eternity, we feel the eternity as long as the vibrations are undergoing the process of becoming permanent (I like to call it "installing vibrations"). As long as we concentrate on the feeling of eternity (or any other center of the meditation) the work of installing the vibrations in the body is in process.

Keeping attention on the energy allows its vibrations to be installed, but the point here is that the actual movement of the energy in or out makes it tangible for us at the moment of the movement. As in sex, we feel when the energy moves; and when a lot of energy moves we feel it stronger.

So we see that with our attention we make the work, and that we *feel* the vibrations only when they come or go (install or uninstall); but there is also the fact that when new energies arrive, they push the old ones out. So we will also feel the ones that leave the body. This is my point: **when old energies leave the body, we feel them as they are,** as the vibrational information they carry, normally unpleasant information.

For example, in the meditation on eternity, around the twenty-five-day point we will feel eternity and enjoy the process, but the more we install the eternity vibrations, the more the opposite vibrations are going out. And all of these, including fears and samskaras, we experience in the same way as when they came in. You can feel that the process of installing new vibrations is successful, because you feel good and you take this good feeling as a sign that the process is going well. But then many imbalanced and unpleasant feelings come to our attention, rising from the bottom (subconsciousness is in the belly, consciousness in the head) and you feel like you have done something wrong and try to deepen the meditation, to catch the feeling; but it does not feel like it did before.

We know that it is the pendulum that goes back and forth and now you see one of the reasons for the existence of this law (the law of rhythm). While "going back" we give our old vibrations time to leave us, and we feel them while they leave. When we experience illness symptoms the energy of the illness is on the way out; when the body is taking measures to fight the illness and the illness (energies) leave the body, we experience this as symptoms. When we are experiencing the old vibrations leaving, there is no need to panic or to think that you have slid back or are doing something wrong: keep going. One day imbalanced and unpleasant feelings will disappear like they never existed, and you will feel clean, different (in a good way), and that is the sign that the installation of the energies and uninstallation of the old ones has been successfully accomplished. The new feeling will become part of you. This means that you are not going to feel eternity all the time; precisely because it is part of you, you will feel it only when it comes or goes.

Get used to it! This feeling of the energies coming and going is natural and necessary. Be patient, don't fight it, don't try to hold whatever is leaving you.

Different people have **different ways** to contact the subtle info. Some of us can easily visualize anything, others can feel everything and so on. As we have five senses in the physical reality, we have the same in the subtle reality. For some of us, some of the subtle senses are more active than others. We have to stick to the instructions of the exercises when we visualize or feel, but we should also bear in mind that we all are sensitive in different ways.

The way in which we receive information from the subtle levels is the way in which we are sensitive. I normally feel the same thing the person in front of me feels (reflection). I have reflections on the state of the aura of the person or any object I put my inner or outer attention on. I have inner feedback that works on the same principle; it's just that in meditation we do it deliberately and for a prolonged time. I can even interpret and understand it better than the person experiencing it.

When I think of things, they appear as intuitional feelings that lack any language of understanding (of the mind) but I know exactly what they mean. Some of you will feel the same way as I do and some will receive information in a different manner; this is absolutely fine. What I need to make clear here is that it is normal for people to have difficulties with a particular exercise. Whatever kind of sensitivity you have, it is the best kind for you to fulfill your path (if one day you decide to take it). Besides, any kind of sensitivity that is related to the five senses can be developed, part of the point of the exercises is to do exactly this.

Do only one thing at a time

Reflex is when your body reacts automatically to something, be it by birth (like the gag reflex) or acquired habit like feeling stressed every time we see that our angry boss is calling us. The same with exercises and energetic work. If you did the candle exercise correctly, every time you think of doing it, you will go to alpha waves right away. I have said this before, but it is very important to do only the exercise and to do it in a specific way as written. If you do it wrong or add modifications or side details, they will become part of the reflex.

Knowing how the reflex works can help us in the future, when we want to create a button that puts us in the desirable state. People who practice astral travel create three level buttons that activate the travel-automatically reflex. But while we are learning, keep to the principle of KISS and avoid creating reflexes.

Another principle that I would like to introduce is the principle of **window to the future.** (This is my name for it.) It goes like this: after fulfilling a certain potential and acquiring emptiness, we are gifted or granted an elevated state. This elevated state opens many small windows full of different notions and good feelings. While this state is in power, we feel like we have received a gift from the universe, something we never worked for but have maybe always wanted. When we feel confident and comfortable in this state the image or experience disappears, leaving us just memories. This is how this book came to exist. I saw it ready and helping people and it felt very good, so I started writing the next day.

A few things to say about this state. First, it tells you where you need to go, what is your direction. For example, during the "experience" you felt very generous and kind (loving, caring or just good at making energetic balls), but your normal state is much less generous and kind, perhaps even the opposite. The universe shows you the next goal. Even if you try to recreate the feeling you won't be able to, because this "spectacle" came from God and God's actions do not leave imprints, they don't leave samskara. This is the second thing to learn about this state.

Third, if we keep working on getting to the place we saw in the "spectacle," in the windows opened to the future, we will reach this stage and it will become permanent. Fourth, we can reach it only if we follow the way that the universe has paved for us. In other words, we cannot pick the route by which we are going to get there.

Each of these sub-principles can be thought of as a principle by itself. At least the last one: **We can pick the destination but not the route.**

The imprint that we have mentioned already, or the lack of it: every time we receive a message that looks so clear and true but which after a while we can't recall, it means this was a message from the universe.

We cannot recall it because it leaves no imprint. Everything we do, we create imprints in reality and in most cases we create karma (good or bad). Only by following the universal will, when God is creating and acting through us, do we leave no imprints. When we say God is acting through us we don't mean the ultimate God but the God particle that is the *true* you. This is the path of love, your personal path of love and service. It is the true you motivated by unconditional love, doing what you love to do and what you do best to make the planet a better place. As my teacher says (and other people's teachers say), you need to live your life so at the end of it you will leave Earth a bit better than it was.

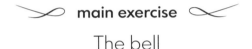

main exercise

The bell

Time and duration
Every day for 15 minutes in total.

What to do
Visualize a bell and move it to three different directions and back, for 5 minutes each.

How to do it
Perform this exercise while standing. Imagine a bell (without the clapper), a big one, the size of your body. Inside the bell there is a sharp cone with the pointed side going down. If you were in the bell you could see the conus pointing at you. Now, using your imagination, take the bell and put it on your head, in such a way that the peak of the conus falls on the pineal gland, as if the bell is standing on your head and the only point of contact is between the peak and the pineal gland (don't concentrate on the physical). You can imagine two handles inside the bell that you can use to lift it.

When the bell is in place, keep your attention on the contact point (all the time, attention, remember?), hold the imaginary handles of the imaginary bell, and start moving the bell back and forth, back and forth. Five minutes. Then left to right and back to the left and so on, five minutes, and at the end clockwise and counterclockwise and so on, five minutes. Fifteen minutes in total.

When you finish, erase the bell.

If you feel very strong activity of the pineal gland, switch the mind to analytical work (in other words, activate the left side of the brain).

Do the candle and the energetic balls exercises, to balance.

What not to do
- Don't imagine anything on the pineal gland or the bell. No symbols and no words, much less faces.
- Don't do the exercise more than it says: five minutes back and forth and five minutes to each side, tops.
- Don't do it close to bedtime.
- Don't look at what leaves your body.
- Don't concentrate on the physical aspect.
- If you have uncontrolled visions in your life and you see stuff— DON'T DO THIS EXERCISE. Find someone to help you learn and manage the visions.

How and when do I know it's working?
At the moment of doing the exercise you can expect to feel like a flower is opening in your head (don't look hard for the flower feeling, it is just an indicator). In the long run, you can expect to feel more energetic, calm, balanced.

Why am I doing it?
This is maybe the most powerful and effective exercise in the book. The pineal gland is a sacral organ that is connected with the seventh chakra. While doing the exercise we awake the pineal gland and

it begins balancing the body and cleansing it of negative energy. It awakes some of your inner energy and helps to open the seventh chakra. The work on the pineal gland switches the body to alpha waves, after which we will feel dizzy or sleepy. The rest of the magical effects of this exercise, I would like to leave you to discover for yourself.

If you cannot do the exercise every day or for fifteen minutes at a time, just do less. Later we will introduce a fears-cleansing practice that will make this exercise more pleasant. Until then, be strong but moderate.

The process of cleansing might be unpleasant. Energies come up and they can carry unpleasant previous experiences. It is very important not to look at what is leaving the body and to do the candle and the energetic balls to calm down some of the effects of the bell exercise.

In short

This exercise is powerful and may make you experience new sensations, but stimulating the awakening of the pineal gland by this method helps to clean and balance the bodies in a very efficient manner. Ring the bell . . .

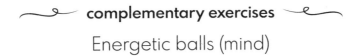

complementary exercises
Energetic balls (mind)

Time and duration

The same as the energetic balls exercise.

What to do

With the mind, compress an energetic ball and move it.

How to do it

Think of the times you have done the energetic balls exercise we have already looked at. Now direct this memory to a spot in the air and let the *prana* turn into a ball of energy. While doing the previous energetic balls exercise you were creating a reflex. If you evoke in your memory the actual ball compression, particularly a moment at which you succeeded very fast, using this reflex from your memory you might be able to compress the energy into a ball just with your mind. If you don't manage this, don't worry; just try your best.

When you have the ball, place it on one of your palms and let it go on the route you already know well: up the hand, behind the neck and down the other arm to the palm. From here, let the ball jump back to the original palm and start again. Do ten circles. Then put the ball on the other palm and repeat: ten circles. Now enlarge the ball to a bigger size and let it enter from the front and leave from the back, then enter from the back and exit from the front. Like swings. Remember how it was done when you did it manually, earlier in the book. Stop it in the midline of the body and let it go up and down that line ten times.

If the ball gets lost, make a new one. If it is hard to make a new one with the mind, compress with the hands, but do try to move with the mind.

Here we finish. Let the ball go; or you can compress it even more, to the size of a ping-pong ball, until it becomes red from compression. Take the ball and insert it in the body under the navel, and let it go to the place you need energy the most.

What not to do

- Don't change the route.
- Don't change the shape; it must be a ball.
- Don't imagine the balls having any particular color.
- Don't use anything but the mind to move the balls.

How and when do I know it's working?
When you have succeeded in creating the balls, and they obey your mind, you will know. At some point the balls will move themselves.

Why am I doing it?
Remember a long time ago, at the beginning of the book, we spoke of the concentration power or willpower, and that we have to build it up so the energies cooperate with our will and you can master them. If you worked hard then, you will see now that they are controlled by you. This will be useful when we come to energetic cleansings later.

In short
Moving the balls with your mind will give you active control over energies.

Tai Chi palms playing

Time and duration
Once a day, 10–15 minutes.

What to do
Close and open.

How to do it
Traditionally, the best time for this exercise is considered to be right after the tai chi standing exercise, but you can do it any time.

Stand in the tai chi standing posture but with the back more concave or arched.

Let the palms touch each other as if you were saying thank you or praying. For a better understanding of the position, let the whole of both forearms touch, from the tips of the fingers to the elbows. Now you can feel how your chest has concaved in and the back is slightly curved backwards. Place the palms at the level of the heart. On the inhale, let the back straighten and raise the head slightly; the knees straighten, the shoulders go back. Like you are a spring that has been pushed down and on the inhale is released.

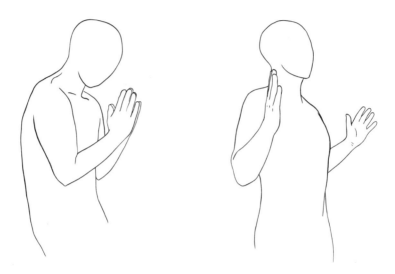

The actual movement comes from four points: neck, knees, lower back and mid-spine. During the movement the palms separate, but only as the consequences of the other moving parts. The palms don't lead the movement, they follow. The mid-spine is pushed in, letting the chest move forward a little and the shoulders back. This movement makes the palms separate. While they grow apart from each other, visualize an energetic wire connecting the fingers at the places where they were touching each other or as if you have chewing gum stuck to your fingers. When the palms move away from each other, the gum gets stretched. At first, concentrate on the visualization of the substance that connects the fingers (gum or energetic wires). Later, when you begin to be able to feel the magnetic field, concentrate on that instead.

When the spring (your body) is stretched and opened up by this movement, the palms go to the sides. During this opening movement we inhale. The movement is as long as the inhale, meaning that the breath duration and the movement have to be synchronized. On the exhale, go back to your original position. This has to be synchronized with the length of the exhale.

You can try starting by just moving the palms on the inhale and exhale, not the whole of the body, to see how it feels; but the full exercise requires all four points to move. Open on the inhale: knees, lower back curved slightly back, mid-spine curving in, shoulders back, moving the hands to the sides and the chin up and down; the head and neck will follow. On the exhale everything moves the other way, starting from the neck and finishing with the knees. Remember, concentrate on the magnetic field between the palms. If you don't feel the field just wait for it; it will come later. Meanwhile, see the chewing gum . . .

What not to do
Don't let your attention wander from the exercise; keep focusing between the palms and try to sense the magnetic energy.

How and when do I know it's working?
You will feel some streams, magnetic fields and pins-and-needles sensations, between and in the palms. When you do feel them, concentrate on them and on the energetic movement in the body. Don't force the movement, let it be natural. There might be moments when you feel the magnetic field but the body does not go further, as if it's stuck. That is okay. Stay in the position and wait.

Why am I doing it?
It opens the channels, increases the amount of energy you can channel, and helps with other exercises; while this one is important for everyone, it is especially valuable for people who would like to

use energy for healing others. It also offers interesting developments for the future.

In short
Use the powerful tai chi standing posture to work with the magnetic field and increase the energy you can channel.

Cobra breathing

Time and duration
Once or twice a day for 3–5 minutes.

What to do
Sit in a comfortable pose and breathe, producing a specific sound.

How to do it
Perform the alternative breathing exercise.

Take your favorite meditation pose. Have your hands with fingers interlocked resting in the lap. Slowly, on the inhale, drop the head back as much as it goes while still feeling relaxed. Let your attention be on your throat, at the center where the soft part of the throat meets with the upper bone of the chest.

Now breathe and listen to the noises that come out. It is like there is less room for the air in the throat, so the air is more concentrated, more compressed. If you cannot hear the sound, place one of your hands on that point on the throat and press it gently. Keep breathing and play with the pressing hand. Press on different spots. We are looking for breathing that makes a kind of snoring sound or as if someone is breathing through a mask with a filter.

At the end, bring your head back on an exhale, slowly and carefully.

If you cannot achieve the desired sound, take the pose known in yoga as cobra *(bhujangasana)* and try to breathe and make the sound while in the pose.

Once you are familiar with the breathing, the sound and the feeling, you can perform it without taking cobra pose or leaning the head back.

Make the inhale and the exhale equally long and in between them, hold the air in or out for a few seconds. You can try this: inhale five seconds, hold three seconds, exhale five seconds. Make the sound on both inhale and exhale. Concentrate on the center point of the throat, above the sternum.

On the last inhale, take the hands to the sides and up, like you are drawing a circle around yourself. Let the hands meet above your head, palms together. While doing this, raise the gaze to the point where the palms meet. These two movements must be done simultaneously. On the exhale, bring the hands down in a straight line and let them stop at the level of the chest (in *anjali mudra*). Stay that way for a few moments.

What not to do
- Don't use your voice to make the sound.
- Don't strain the throat.

How and when do I know it's working?
This breathing can be performed during an ordinary hatha yoga practice. This way of breathing awakens the fire element; our chest and throat become hot. This heat is caused by the movement of the energy through our body. When you feel the heat you know it's working.

Why am I doing it?
This exercise awakens the *kundalini* (at some level: see below) and brings it up the spine. When the *kundalini* awakens it balances and cleanses the body and the energetic centers (including balancing the masculine and the feminine energies). We already know that

we have energetic bodies and of course the physical one. First we must cleanse the physical body, through cleansing, physical exercise and later by keeping to the right diet. Then we can proceed to the subtle bodies. The first one to put into balance is the emotional, then the mental body. While balancing and cleansing those bodies we acquire the right understanding, behavior and habits. We become calmer and better people (hopefully).

Kundalini is the energetic stream running from the root of our spine to the crown of the head. By working on our mental and emotional bodies we are improving *kundalini* flow and helping the stream of energy to reach a higher state. The full awakening of the *kundalini* happens when it reaches the highest (crown) chakra, once the whole set of bodies and chakras are balanced. But this *kundalini* energy is always moving up the spine, regardless of whether or not we have yet reached the point of it being awakened.

According to the principle of correspondence—"as above so below"—we have basic structures that repeat themselves. The solar system has the structure of one star in the middle and the rest of the stars moving around it. Up a level, we see that our galaxy and the universe itself have the same structure. Down again, we see that the atom has the same structure. Each of our cells contains the whole DNA code. When we meditate, inside us we can reach whatever is outside us. The same principle applies to the chakras; if we decide we are going with the most well-known seven chakras system, every chakra has seven sub-chakras that reflect the same structure of the "main" seven chakras. And going further up, all seven chakras are sub-chakras of one chakra of a higher plane of us that also has seven chakras. Of course the same is true of the bodies. Each body has sub-bodies. From this book we know about four: the physical, etheric, emotional and mental. But normally in esoteric practice we like to have seven of everything. So all the bodies, or energetic planes, or levels of consciousness are seven, and each has seven sub-planes.

This book is all about understanding the role of subtle structure and balancing it. Every exercise is designed either to give you the tools or to balance your bodies. After you finish the book, you will know enough essential information to achieve balance. There is no need to give more information about the *kundalini* here than that already given. If you are on a spiritual development path this energy will accompany you at each level and beyond the bodies described here.

In short

Awaken the inner fire using the cobra breathing to activate cleansing and achieve balance.

Breathe (sniff) as dogs do

Time and duration

Once a day for as long as you can.

What to do

Sniff like a dog.

How to do it

You must be sitting to do this exercise. And be mindful not to do it too intensively at the beginning.

Perform the alternative breathing exercise.

When you have finished, concentrate on the nose—the nose only. Start breathing in a way that makes your nostrils move. When you inhale they suck in, on the exhale they flare out. Remember how dogs' noses move when they excitedly sniff stuff? Like that.

The breathing has to be rhythmical, inhale and exhale equal. They can be long or short; that does not matter at this point, whatever is comfortable for you—but they must be equal.

You want to get to the point where you feel like you are only a nose. There is nothing but the nose and the process of sniffing (breathing).

During the process try to relax; don't resist if you feel some energy leaving the body. Be relaxed. Let it flow.

What not to do
Don't do this while standing or lying down.

How and when do I know it's working?
You will feel lighter afterwards, a kind of emotional relief.

Why am I doing it?
During this exercise, as with the previous ones, we cleanse our energetic bodies and awake inner energies and balance them.

In short
Relieve energetic and emotional blockages by "sniffing."

5

Energy Management

For modern people the word "energy" is associated with fuel. We need energy to keep going. But let us try to understand it more broadly, for a wider perspective. There are many kinds of energies. We have seen that vibrations define the quality of the energy. We use the term energy because God is energy, God is always in motion and so are we, and so is everything around us. Everything is energy. The more you deepen your understanding of the subtle realities the more you come to realize this.

What is so important about energy that it has to be managed? Two aspects are of very high importance to sensitives: amount and clarity. In other words, we need to have enough energy and this energy has to be compatible with our own energy.

We have talked about methods of stealing energies and how we waste our energy on negative emotions and false beliefs. Let us elaborate on that.

The most classic case of giving energy is paying attention; we feed what we look at, be it people, objects or situations outside, or our worries, fears, happiness, joy or just thoughts on the inside. People with energetic deficiency who are using this strategy keep your attention linked to them. After they have caught your attention they hold it against your will; even after the conversation is over and you are on your way, they are still linked to you. It's true: the connection is not broken.

Those people do it because they need energy, but they do a disservice to themselves. The best thing for each person is to live on their own energies. This is the aspect of clarity. For us and for every person on the planet, the best thing is to use our own energies. Energies have vibrations and those vibrations are the character of the energy. Each of us have our own character, intentions, subtle processes that are imprinted on our energy. When we take or give energy we do it with the whole package of characteristics and imprints. My energy is not good for you and yours is not good for me.

Those connections are not made only by conversation or energy-stealing. We pass on the street and our subtle bodies touch—we exchange energy. We pass by tens of people a day—we have tens of different imprints on our subtle bodies (aura). We pass through clouds of emotions and people's thoughts, we visit rooms and buildings with energy of a negative character. We come in contact with people on a physical level. We think about people. All our interactions are an exchange of energies.

Crazy, huh? Now you start to realize how much your sensitivity absorbs like a sponge, how much you actually feel. Even after the action is done, you still feel the energies of others on and in you. But there is an easy solution: don't panic.

Our goal is to have today more energy than we had yesterday and to keep our energy clean of others'. There is an endless quantity of energy around us; unmanifested energy that does not have an imprint. We pass through this energy all the time. When you are inside it, it covers everything. The centers of your chakras are drinking in this energy, processing it and distributing it to the relevant areas in the body. You breathe, eat and drink this energy—we call it *prana,* as we have seen already.

When we meditate, do the tai chi standing posture, the wheel of power, energetic balls exercise, etheric hands, pole of light and the bell, we accumulate energy. All are energy-bringing or channel-opening exercises (sometimes both). At this point, you already have a clear notion of how energy feels while you are doing those exercises. You know how to bring more energy into your system. We will keep working on the balance so this energy won't be wasted on negative emotions or thoughts or stolen by others. At this point these negative thoughts and emotions have to be reduced significantly. We just have to learn how to cleanse unwanted energies (basically everything but our own energies) and to understand that sharing or giving energies is not such a good idea.

Living with your own energies is essential. Sharing or giving them would be like receiving our own medicine in hospital and deciding to share or exchange that. Of course there are some moments at which we have to be in resonance with other people; we like to be physically engaged and spend time with people we love and care for. We want to meet people who inspire us, we want to live a connected life.

You need to pay attention to your links with other people and with yourself. Do you drink others' energy? Who are those in your life who take your energy? Why do you think you give it to them? How do you justify giving them energies? Energy management is a conscious process; you have to be aware of the situation.

When people take our energy we rarely feel it at the same moment. When we have a nice conversation with someone who is in some kind of need, during the conversation we feel useful; but at some point or after the conversation, we feel tired and low or down. Why do we feel this if we have had a good conversation that made us feel "encouraged"? If you reflect on this feeling, you will discover that it happens every time someone takes your energy, because it is a deceptive encouragement that comes from outside, not from within us. The same feeling comes when we are drunk. Every idea sounds so reasonable and "encouraging." If you know how to spot this false "encouragement" you will be able to recognize on the spot when your energy is taken away.

This is how it feels when you are being used for energies or the energies of others have left their imprint on yours. There is a feeling of "justified victim" that we enjoy at the moment of the act, but which just makes us feel weak later.

Think about *pity* and *anger,* two of the emotions people provoke in you. This takes your energy. Think of an angry argument (it doesn't matter if you won or lost it). Or a person you help or give money to because they have made you pity them.

Maybe you are friend-zoning someone to get his attention and energy, or you yourself are in someone's friend zone because they suck your energy. Meanwhile you act like you want to please them; in other words, you look for their approval. Maybe your parents or bosses always keep you in the state of feeling that they are not satisfied with you. Do you cooperate? Do you believe their opinion matters, and do you try to gain their approval of your actions and choices? If yes, you are a slave—free yourself. Only you matter. If you believe you are a good worker or that following the heart and not the head is the right path for you, walk on your path. You don't need anyone's approval. Even if you are mistaken and the path you picked was wrong, still, it is your lesson and the decision is yours. People who surround and love us can help us realize what we want, what is right and what is good for us, but should never force us or make us seek their approval.

Believe in your own freedom, your integrity and capacities. No one has the right to enslave others' will. We are free creatures. This is, from my point of view, the first and most important law of the universe: *free will and the right to choose.* No true healer, spiritual or esoteric teacher will help you if it is against your will or your well-being.

Freedom has a much broader meaning too: it is all the notions you subject yourself to.

For example: To be a good Catholic means not to enjoy sex (on the dotted lines you can put any two words that describe you). We have these beliefs we have never examined and we are subject to them; they imprison us. It doesn't mean you have to disobey or revolutionize everything—if you think that your actions are the right ones, keep doing them—but don't subject yourself to the belief that stands behind them. On the path of the spiritual seeker we discover that there are universal laws that no one taught us in school. These laws might come into conflict with our inner system of laws, which for most of us has been acquired over our lifetime and reflects social norms and beliefs. The core of our inner system of laws is acquired from birth until we are about five, when we take everything the grown-ups tell us as truth.

Later, social and government systems add other layers of information. When we encounter the spiritual laws, we see them through the prism of our original system. The interesting thing is, we will most certainly examine and question the spiritual system of laws (or any other new system we meet) but never the original one. Where does this get problematic? First, if we consider our original system to be a fundamental belief, not a relative set of rules. When we believe something is fundamental, we subjugate ourselves to it; but in reality, we are free souls with free will.

Second, when government or social law act in a way that is in conflict with spiritual laws. It is right, of course, to keep public order and to be an honest person. But the key is not to let notions of social or government law have power over your soul. Just as you should not give other people, ideas or bacteria or viruses power over you. You are free by default, in the same way as you have love in your heart by default. No one can take it from you—as long as you don't let them.

This brings us to control. When we try to control something, be it a person, animal or situation, we waste a lot of energy. Trying to change the course of something or impose our will on someone is wrong and wasteful. This is also related to free will. If you want your kid not to do something, speak to their heart and mind but don't force control on them.

Think about all those people who control you and those whom you control. How much energy it takes to keep the people you control in the state or behavior you want. Control is not the answer; find a way to inspire or make a point. If it does not work, pray: "May the best happen to . . ." and then leave it alone.

If you control people you accept the idea of control in general, and this makes you vulnerable to the control of others or to control you enforce on yourself. Maybe you have a fear of losing control or fear of others controlling you? Think about it.

After making the connection, strengthening it, when the inner connection is strong enough, your heart will tell you what to direct your energies to. The heart's language is passion, desire and enthusiasm. The wish to serve others and to make this world better by contributing your God's particle, your part of love.

 main exercise

Inner connection meditation

Time and duration
Once a day for 20 minutes for 40 days.

What to do
Take your favorite pose for meditation, go to trance, see yourself as a baby, love yourself and let yourself love you back.

How to do it
Take your pose for meditation, put on protections and gradually relax up to the point at which you don't feel your body, your surroundings or any other limits. There is only bodiless you. When you

feel it is the right time, think that you are in the heart (not the physical one), and see yourself as a baby, as small as possible, a few weeks after birth or even a few days. See how cute and calm you are, how wise and balanced. This is you coming back from adventures in the higher realms to the Earthly life to learn new lessons. How do you feel towards the baby? If you feel love, let this feeling grow and take over you, let it come to every cell of your body. Let it come to your head and become a part of your thinking; see the world from the perspective of love. After twenty minutes, come back to reality but keep the feeling. Turn off the protection and keep enjoying the nice feeling of love.

The answer to the question "How do you feel towards the baby?" is very important and might bring some understanding into your life. Needless to say, whatever you feel towards the baby is how you feel and see yourself. Any feeling that is negative or heavy has to be cleansed. If you have deeper issues with yourself, solve them as soon as possible.

The feeling that you have to feel is love. You have to feel love towards the baby and feel that it loves you. If you feel nothing, send love to the baby. If you cannot send love, think of someone who loves you and direct their love to the baby and yourself. If you cannot, go beyond the baby, go further back. Tell yourself "go to the moment at which I was connected" (just remember to come back).

When you are connected to yourself, it also means you are connected to God; you feel the stream of love. Everything we create has some built-in modules or features. We also have some built-in features and one of them is the connection with God, with love. We cannot be disconnected from the source. This connection is in the heart and we feel it as a stream of love. This connection cannot be taken from us; we might forget it exists but it is always there. And when we say, "you are disconnected from yourself and God" (which are the same), we mean you have forgotten about this connection. This exercise is about reminding you, about bringing the vibrations of this connection back into your life. Love is always in our heart; its stream is there. We can give it the shape of a flame or light and observe it.

What not to do
Don't worry if you don't feel love; it is there, we just need to find it.

How and when do I know it's working?
You feel the love.

Why am I doing it?
To remember your connection with God and bring this love into your life. You live in a reality guided by the information and the beliefs you keep in your head. The head can perfectly calculate everything (at best) but never has the whole picture. Even if it did, the head does not know how to want or desire. The head is a great tool but it cannot tell you what to want. Mind is a good servant but a bad master, as the old proverb says. The mind, the head, does not provide real guidance, the guidance that is on your side and knows better than you. When you bring the vibrations of this inner love back to your life, you start to re-evaluate everything. With time you find the things you love and want. You come to a place you were always aiming to reach but never could. Now you are there, looking at the world from this perspective, from the perspective of your true self.

Connecting to the heart gives us access to higher means of communication and receiving information. Many times we have an instinct, or gut feelings, that mistakenly we call intuition. The language of intuition in fact begins here; intuition is a complex understanding, not just the feeling of right or wrong.

In short
Connect with yourself as a baby, love yourself. Use the love that is always in your heart by seeing it as a flame or a light.

⟡ complementary exercises ⟡
See the world as it is

Time and duration
Any time, for a couple of minutes.

What to do
See the world as it is.

How to do it
Take a moment and stop all your thoughts and engagements. Raise your head and look at the street; look what is going on there. Now turn off your imprint, turn off the habit of forcing yourself on reality, the one you always do to see the world from your perspective, through your eyes. Turn it off and see the world through the eyes of yourself if your energy had never influenced the picture you are watching. Look at things like you never influence them. Turn off your judgement, see things as not good or bad but as they are.

Try to reach this state even if it takes time. Keep trying. If you cannot succeed after a few attempts, leave it and come back later. After you have succeeded, keep looking at the world with this attitude: zero influence, zero judgement, absolutely neutral.

What not to do
Don't get scared; you still exist, you are just not influencing the world but are a bystander.

How and when do I know it's working?
When you see the world differently and you have this inner feedback that you are free from controlling the reality you live in.

Why am I doing it?

We don't pay attention to our interactions with the world and its planes. We have got used to planning everything in advance, going on automatically without questioning our influence and interaction with the world. We do not see this as automatic action but as free will and sometimes as samskara. When we plan something we are already sending a part of our will to reality so that it will be designed for us when we reach this stage. We are too entangled with the reality—release it, let it go, be free. Be free of control and judgement. See what comes into your life instead of control and judgement, fear, entanglement and imprints.

When you are able to disconnect from it, you will be free and relieved. Everything you influence is influencing you back. You cannot control and not be controlled, you cannot judge everything and not judge yourself.

In short

See the world without coloring it with your thoughts and emotions so you start to see things as they really are.

A walk in the park

Time and duration

While you are already on your way somewhere on foot.

What to do

Release the body to lead itself.

How to do it

When you're walking somewhere (it's better if you are not in a rush), gradually release control over your body and its actions; just let it keep going with you as the observer. If it is fighting with you, don't let it; gradually, like taking off an old and annoying sticker, bit by a bit, give up control and let the body do whatever it wants. It will keep going to the original destination—probably—but it will pick its own rhythm. It is fun, you will like it.

What not to do
Don't panic when you succeed.

How and when do I know it's working?
When you become an outside observer of your bodies' actions and let the body walk by itself.

Why am I doing it?
We micromanage everything and it is unhealthy and exhausting. We can trust our body to fulfill its actions without our close control. Step by step release everything, all the actions your body knows how to do, things it can do while you are offline, while you're not trying to control it.

In short
Relax and discover that your body is in control, and that its memory is useful and you can trust it.

Involuntary breathing

Time and duration
A few times a day for a couple of minutes a time.

What to do
Sit and watch yourself breathe.

How to do it

Find a moment when you have nothing urgent to do. Sit in a quiet corner. Take a few deep inhales and exhales, very slowly. When you feel calmer, disengage yourself from the breathing and let it be an involuntary process. Just watch how your body performs this act. If your body wants to take deep breaths or to breathe short and fast, let it do whatever it wants. Without your intervention and control it will find its natural balance. You just have to learn to watch without control and without taking over.

What not to do

Don't pay too much attention to the process; let it be easy.

How and when do I know it's working?

When you stop having urges to adjust your breathing or to take control over it and are comfortable with the breathing as it is.

Why am I doing it?

The element of control is huge in our lives, but by controlling everything, we control things we are not supposed to. When we let go of control and pass it to the higher realms, we feel calmer and more natural.

In short

We do not need to interfere with our body's functions. When we observe the body like this we gain new trust and new connection with it.

Note: In martial arts the body is trained. At the beginning the brain is present; later it is absent. In combat the brain has to be absolutely absent. The moment you think, you have lost.

Emotions cleansing

Time and duration

Once every few weeks or when needed.

What to do

Burn the negativity from the emotions and balance them.

How to do it

Make a list of some of the emotions you want to cleanse; let us say three strong and three weak emotions.

Make sure no one and nothing will interrupt the process. Reserve around one hour and try not to schedule anything for straight afterwards. If you want to, do the bell, energetic balls and candle exercises before performing this one; they will help you keep concentration for a longer period of time and stay in alpha waves longer and deeper.

Take up a posture in which you will be comfortable throughout the whole process; your meditation or relaxation posture perhaps.

Go to trance and put in protections; ask your inner guide, your higher self and the angels to assist you in this process and protect you. Ask them to prevent you doing harm to yourself, to help you cleanse the emotions and balance them. Ask from the heart.

When you are in trance, the protections are in place and you feel they have heard your prayer, tell yourself "I am in the heart," then tell yourself to go to your place. Don't expect anything; the place that appears is the place. It is your inner place and no one else can be there; if you do meet someone there ask your angels or your God for them to be removed from there without causing you any harm.

Now see yourself in your place. Not from outside but as you see the world, from the eyes out. Sit in your meditative posture and ask the pole of light to come and surround you. Feel the protection of it, how it is cleansing you and removing all the negative things while also healing where it is necessary. When you feel ready, let your mind surf down the pole of light and see yourself in an elevator, going down one level. When the doors open you see a round room, maybe in the style of an old Mayan temple (or anything else you like), in the middle of which there is an open fireplace but no fire.

Sit facing the fireplace, take the flame from your heart and light the fire in the fireplace. See its colors, feel its warmth; in general, enjoy the atmosphere. Now take one of the emotions from your list and pass it through the fire. But do it gradually. You can recollect the emotion, or just think "Here I am taking this emotion from my body and passing it through the fire."

Let the fire burn the negativity out of the emotion and balance it with love. When the emotion is cleansed, put it back. Ask the angels to assist you in understanding and putting the emotion into balance in your real life. When the emotion passes through the fire, be relaxed; whatever burns, release it, let it go.

After you have performed the same cleansing for all the emotions on your list, thank the fire and bring it back to the heart. Feel how it feels to have it back. Take the elevator back to your inner place. When you get there, see the pole of light. Let it charge you, cleanse you and balance you. After you have finished, thank the pole and release it. Look around at your place one last time. You will come here again in the future many times, and you have already been here many times in the past.

Before coming back to reality, make sure that you have completely left the round room and no part of you is left there. When you are ready, gradually come back to reality. Pay attention to your body and your surroundings, come back to the physical. Thank the angels, your inner guide and your higher self. Remove the protections.

What not to do

- Don't do this cleansing if you are not comfortable about using the pole of light, going to trance and successfully coming back.
- Don't leave your mind in your place or in the round room.
- Don't overload yourself; if you notice that after cleansing one or two emotions you are getting tired, come back.
- If one of the emotions was entangled with another emotion, like fear, and the fear does not let you cleanse the emotion, leave it and proceed to the next. Just remember that those two emotions are entangled.

How and when do I know it's working?

You will see that you are not acting in the same way as you used to; the emotions will just come and nothing negative will follow.

Why am I doing it?

Sensitive people, especially, are prone to "collecting" energies from other people. Cleansing emotions brings us back to where we were before we accumulated or collected those negative "attachments." We are not just free from them, but also have the opportunity to see who we are without those "attachments."

In short

Cleanse your emotions so you can see and feel yourself again. You will lose those attachments that are not yours, leaving you with enough energy to balance those that are.

6

~~~~~
~~~~~
~~~~~

Alpha Waves

Just as our reality has different levels of existence, so does our brain work with different levels or waves. The two that concern us are alpha and beta waves. We know that an ordinary person is in the beta wave state most of the time. As we know, alpha waves provide sensitive people with an extra channel of information. Most of the time this information is about other people's feelings and emotions; but while in alpha waves, while going on with your day, we are not deep in the alpha waves and thus receive information on both alpha and beta channels. But if we become engaged with activities more related to physical matters, or activities for which the left hemisphere of the brain is responsible, we switch to beta waves and all the information coming from the alpha waves is, so to speak, turned off. There is nothing bad or negative about beta waves, just as there is nothing bad about the left side of the brain. The problem is imbalance; to work with the left brain only all the time is harmful, and to be in the beta wave state all the time is also not the best thing for us as we miss a huge part of the reality. We perceive the creation differently if we look at the world from the beta waves state than we do from alpha waves. The physical world is perceived through the beta waves and the subtle worlds through the alpha. Both are needed and both are essential. Ultimately, we live in a physical world, and so we need the beta; but we are spiritual creatures, and some of us are sensitive spiritual creatures, so we need the alpha waves too.

This subtle part of reality we can access by switching our brain to alpha waves, which is where, among other things, our subconsciousness lies, or at least where, from this state, we can access it. Every time we prepare to meditate we are making efforts to go to the alpha waves state. When our pineal gland is activated we go to this state, and before we fall asleep, or at the point in the day when we become sleepy. Sometimes you can go to the alpha state very quickly simply by standing near someone with whom you have good resonance who is also engaged in esoteric practices.

The reality we access in the alpha waves state has many advantages and potential hazards. Our subtle senses operate at this level; so, if we know how, we can communicate with subtle creatures, like angels or our beloved friends and relatives who have passed away, and with all that lives in the subtle worlds. All our psychic abilities are developed and put into action from this place. Many gurus and masters are in this state all the time and are merging consciousness with subconsciousness. This is how and from where they see the past and the future, and get in touch with the upper worlds and other dimensions.

This is what I call the *open* stage of subconsciousness, when events, energies and creatures can easily access your subconsciousness. This is an unprotected state for imbalanced people and those who are energetically weak (this is why it is important to use protections).

At this level we are more receptive, for both better and worse. The worse is vulnerability; our traumas can more easily come back and affect us in this state and are more easily triggered. The better is the ability to cleanse our traumas, fears and emotions. From here we can program our mind. Remember the mental body, the way we think we live; it operates on vibrations we call thoughts, on the same principle as the emotional body operates on the experiences we call emotions. We tend to see emotional reactions as involuntary and mental ones as conscious activity, but in fact both are subject to previous programming "saved" in our subconsciousness. The alpha waves state is the key to accessing this subconsciousness and this is why all deep cleansing exercises require us to be in meditative state.

This is the reason why we have to be relaxed (in the alpha state) when doing yoga, healing, meditation and other energetic exercises. Their effect is stronger when we are at this level; the imprint on our subtle energies is faster and deeper. This is why when you do these practices, you should make sure you put in protections, or make sure your instructor does. With time, though, if you keep exercising, you won't need them.

After major, life-changing events that require us to have a broader channel of information (like giving birth, or having a traumatic experience like bereavement or losing a job and income), we may discover that our intuition has become stronger. At the same time we may always feel worried and find that new fears come into our lives, fears that are not always obviously related to the event. The reason is that our brain has switched to the alpha waves state; in some ways this is important and useful—for example, it helps new mothers to feel the connection with the needs of their baby—but along with this come the opened, unprotected aspects of being in the alpha state; so the new mother may also become exposed to unreasonable fears and oversensitivity.

Sometimes we might meditate for what feels like hours but when we come back to reality we find that it only lasted for twenty or thirty minutes. And daydreaming feels like tens of minutes while we are doing it; but after coming back to reality, we tend to discover that we were daydreaming for a few minutes at most. The reason is that in the alpha state the flow of time is much slower, so we experience time differently.

Our energy consumption in the alpha state is very low compared to when in the beta waves state. We can stay in the alpha state all day and feel zero tiredness. It is like being in a dream state for the whole day. By contrast, a few hours of beta work—thinking, planning, calculating—take much more energy.

The alpha state is where all our positive and negative past experiences, and most important traumas, live (or at least it is from where they can be accessed). The more "garbage" we have here, the worse is our communication with the subtle realities. Every student of spiritual development or esoteric practices has to start their journey by cleansing this space, and so that is what we are going to do now.

Subconsciousness is the place to which all our knowledge passes. When we learn how to drive, as an example, we are conscious, in the process. But once we know how, this knowledge turns into a skill and moves to our subconsciousness. The subconsciousness contains the knowledge and the skill connected with every event and every craft we have ever learned, including in our previous incarnations.

Let us look back at the methods of getting to the alpha state we already know: morning candle: looking at the aura of a candle flame, defocused vision, slow and deep breathing, relaxation, seeing the field; and the bell exercise, moving the upper part of the body in circles synchronized with the breathing while seated. Think of one of them, the one you have practiced the most, and recall how you are able to reach the alpha state in seconds. When we do something for quite a while, it begins to works automatically, if we simply think of it. You can use this method to go to the alpha state any time you want. To come back, just think of something like your boss at work, your to-do list, or conscious breathing.

It is very important to develop the ability—or in other words, to train—to be in this state for as long as needed. When we sleep we pass through this stage, so it is very difficult for the mind, in the beginning, not to fall asleep. You may well know from your own experience how meditating while lying down can make you fall asleep. The more you do the candle exercise, exert strong willpower and "fight" falling asleep, the more able you will become to stay in this state. And this state has levels. So the stronger your "willpower muscle" is, the deeper you will be able to go and stay awake. It will feel like your body is asleep but your consciousness is awake.

It is very important not to improvise while going to the meditative state. We know very little about this world and the creatures that live there can take advantage of us. People with big egos can be an easy victim to those creatures. They can wear any image they like, whichever one will impress you, and appear like someone who has come to help and support.

I strongly recommend not to go to the meditative state for the sake of "sightseeing," or to try to find your inner guide, read the akashic records, contact angels or otherwise look for wisdom or guidance. Keep the exercise simple. You already know how this part of your existence is influencing your life and how big is its role. Remember, as we have said, free will is the first basic law of the universe. No light creature will volunteer to come and help you in the subtle realms. If you want stuff you have to ask for it. And even then, you don't know who is going to come and "offer" its services. Remember, only negative creatures of the subtle realms volunteer to "help."

However, if you have been "adventurous" enough to go there without your inner guide and you have got stuck with negative creatures, you can use your willpower to get rid of them. If that does not work, invoke the pole of light and imagine this is pure love that surrounds you. And ask the creature to leave you, in the name of God. It sounds so "Catholic Church movies," but it is absolutely true. They run away when they hear about God.

By the way, if you go there and ask your inner guide to appear, someone will always appear. If you have ego issues, this someone will look magnificent and your ego will inflate even more. We see this notion all the time in our culture; in myths and fairy tales, imaginary creatures are normally ill-natured beasts or souls that take advantage of you. Those will appear to every inexperienced and green "alpha traveler" and at the moment we don't have the tools to identify and deal with them. To reach your true inner guide you have to be free from ego (in the sense that we understand ego) and be very balanced. Love has to be part of you. In short, when you go to alpha, don't mess up.

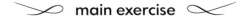

main exercise

Subconsciousness cleansing

Time and duration
As many times and for as long as needed.

What to do
Go to a temple for emotional cleansing and cleanse the dirt.

How to do it
As I say, we had to begin with this exercise. But it is weird, unbelievable and requires some abilities (like the ability to be in the alpha-waves state and not fall asleep). Normally, it is done with your master guiding you and supporting you with their energies and protections. But from the start of this book we have been doing everything possible to prepare you so you can do it by yourself. Many steps of this cleansing are similar to the emotions-cleansing exercise, so you will recognize and perhaps be easily able to do them.

Make a full list of your fears, emotional pains, guilt, regrets (about what you did or did not do) and resentments (remember the emotions entangled with fears from the emotional cleansing).

Try to go back in your memory and add to the list everything you can remember that is related. Go online and find some lists of "fear of . . ." to see which of the fears resonate with you, and put them in the list. Most probably the list you come up with now won't be your full list of fears; many of the things we need to cleanse can be so deep. If you keep doing the bell exercise you will get there. It is advisable to work it out consciously throughout this exercise using the list you have prepared.

This exercise is very energy-consuming, so ensure that you have nothing serious planned for afterwards. Don't start on it if you are tired; save it for a day off or the weekend. We won't be able to cleanse everything this first time; you simply don't have enough energetic resources. So pick out some of the things you resonate most with—no more than seven.

Make sure no one and nothing will interrupt the process. Reserve around one hour for it. If you want, you can help yourself by performing the bell exercise, energetic balls and candle. These will help you to get to a deeper alpha state and stay concentrated.

Find a posture in which you will be comfortable throughout the whole process; your meditation or relaxation pose would be ideal.

Go to trance and invoke protections; ask your inner guide, your higher self and the angels that help you to assist you in this process and protect you. Ask them to prevent you doing harm to yourself and to cleanse and balance the emotions.

When you are in trance, the protections are in place and you feel they have heard your prayer, tell yourself you are in the heart, then tell yourself to go to your place. Don't expect anything; the place that appears is the place. It is your inner place and no one else can be there, so if you meet someone there ask your angels or God to remove them without causing you any harm.

When you are alone and everything is settled, see yourself in your place. Not from the outside but as you see the world—through your eyes. Sit there in your meditative posture and ask the pole of light to come and surround you. Feel the protection of it, how it is cleansing you and removing all the negative things, as well as healing where necessary. When you are done and feel ready, let your mind surf down the pole of light and see yourself in an elevator, going down one level. When the doors open you see a round room, perhaps in the style of an old Mayan temple, or anything else that speaks to you, in the middle of which there is an open well containing clear water.

Sit facing the well and take the first article on your list out of your body (let us say it is fear of being infiltrated by other people's energy). When you take out this fear, it appears as an energetic ball. Command the energy to turn into a paper photo and observe the photo. There might be an image there related to the fear you are cleansing, or it could be just a color; for many people it's a dark one. Now command the photo to burn and throw the ashes into the well. Look at the water. Is it black or gray? Or another color? At the edge of the well there is a pedal; step on it and see the water flush like a toilet, until the water is clear again. At this stage you may feel something leaving your body and feel emptiness or a lack of heaviness. All these are indicators that the energy of the fear has successfully left your subconsciousness.

Take the same fear from your list and do the same procedure again. Monitor the photo and the color of the water in the well after you throw the ashes there. These are your indicators. Once the picture and the water are clean, think about the situation in which the fear was very strong. See if the fear still resonates inside. If yes, keep cleansing. If no, after we have removed the fear, there will be an empty space in the energetic fields; ask for the empty space to be closed.

⁓

Perform the same procedure for every article on your list. If you feel that you are getting tired before you have finished the list, stop and go back to reality.

⁓

After you have performed the same cleansing for all the articles on your list, go back to the elevator and return to your place. When you get there, see the pole of light. Let it charge you, cleanse you and balance you. After you have finished, thank the pole and release it. Look around at your place one last time. You will come here again in the future many times, and you have already been here many times in the past.

Before coming back to reality, make sure that you have completely left the temple or room, that no part of you is left there. When you are ready, gradually come back to reality. Pay attention to your body and your surroundings, come back to the physical. Thank the angels and inner guide, and your higher self.

What not to do
- Don't do this cleansing if you are not completely comfortable about the pole of light, going to trance and successfully coming back.
- Don't leave your mind down there, neither in your place nor in the round room.
- Don't overload yourself; if you are getting tired, come back.

How and when do I know it's working?
When you feel no fear or other kind of emotion in a situation when it normally appears.

Why am I doing it?

This is part of the cleansing of the subconsciousness space. All the subtle creatures that want to support you, all the messages sent to you from the universe and the channel to yourself and God were full of negative energies because of the "garbage." After cleansing the subconsciousness, you can have a calmer life because fewer things will trigger negative energies. Your intuition will become more vivid and the energetic flow be stronger. It is similar to finding the right radio station that has no background noise or static.

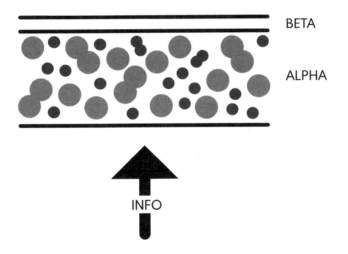

In short

Cleanse your subconsciousness of unwanted emotions and use the released energy for better things.

Note: Whenever you have come to the end of your full list of fears, emotional pains, guilt, regrets and resentments, do a general cleansing. First tell yourself, "Now I am taking out all the fears I have not cleansed yet." Then do the same for emotional pains, guilt, regrets and resentments.

⟿ complementary exercise ⟾
Organs, etheric hands, and emotions

Time and duration
As long as it takes and as many times as needed.

What to do
Use your etheric hands to direct energy to your organs and go to trance to see the feedback.

How to do it
Note: In this exercise we use the etheric hands to touch the etheric equivalents of the organs, not the physical organs. All the organ names mentioned thus refer to etheric, not physical organs. This is very important.

⸻

If you have been training your etheric hands and feel confident about using them, this should be fairly easy. If not, return to this exercise after you have trained the etheric hands for a while and feel them steady and stable.

Sit comfortably, straight spine, hands on the belly at the level of the solar plexus with one on each side, not touching each other. Raise your etheric hands above the physical. Put the etheric hands together palm to palm. Bend the fingers ninety degrees. Place this structure on the body, four fingers under the navel. Keep it there for a while, keeping your attention on the space between the etheric hands.

Now take the etheric hands and put them into the spleen. Let the energy flow and fill the spleen. Let it start pushing out the old energies (it might take a while for this process to begin). As you breathe in, visualize white *prana* flowing from the nose into the spleen and charging it with energies. On the exhale, let the old energy leave through the nose. When you feel ready, take the etheric hands out and put them back into the physical hands.

Go to trance and be alert to what images might appear. Think of the spleen. Let images and memories of the old energies of the spleen fill your imagination. Be passive and receptive. Those images are part of the suppressed emotions that you have forgotten about. Now they are back in your awareness, if you are confident about the feedback you received from the energy stored in the organ, you can cleanse it by using subconsciousness cleansing as in the previous exercise.

Repeat the exercise with the lungs, kidneys, liver, stomach, thyroid (be very gentle here), bladder, navel, solar plexus, heart, brain, genitals (including ovaries and testicles), hipbones and femurs (one at a time). These are mandatory; after that you can work with any organ or bone you like, do the same with each of the seven main chakras. You can easily find illustrations of them online and in books, but the locations they show are approximate. Use your intuition to find the correct location in your body. The chakras are located in the spine and project themselves to the front and to the back. Work from the front.

What not to do
- If emotions arise but are very difficult to release using the method we have learned, give it time or ask for professional help. Learn and understand the reasons and the value of the emotions. Learn to use them in the right way.
- This is a process; it needs time. Work only on one emotion at a time.
- Don't work on the physical organs but on their energetic doubles.

How and when do I know it's working?
You will feel the emotions rising, then you will cleanse them. The normal flow of energy will be re-established. You will feel yourself acting differently, not like you used to act.

Why am I doing it?

For fun! And also to be healthy and because it is a nice and educational experience. By receiving this kind of feedback, we can know what kind of energetic information is stored there. And later we can choose to cleanse this energy, to be balanced and think with the heart (and intuition) and not with either hidden or known emotional traumas.

In short

Use your etheric hands to stimulate the energetic flow in the organs to engage and manifest their hidden information.

A diary

Time and duration

Every evening.

What to do

Keep a diary of good and less good points in the day, and alternatives.

How to do it

Every evening, write down all the points of the day at which you did not like your behavior. Have a special diary or notebook dedicated only to that purpose. Even after all those cleansings we have done, we still have our behavioral samskaras. Many of them have been cleansed in the meditations and the emotional cleansings, but some of our behavioral ways and reflexes are still in place. And more than that, sometimes we feel that we have not done enough or have done too much of something (imbalanced behavior).

This is the place for us to fix that. Keeping a diary has two purposes: to communicate with our higher self (channeling) or to communicate with our subconsciousness. Here we use it for the second purpose. Writing brings us to the alpha state; but we can also get to a deeper state of alpha by using some of the methods we already know.

Together with the description of the situation and the reaction of yours you did not like, write down three alternative ways of reacting, the ways in which you would like yourself to react. Those three alternative reactions are actually reprogramming your subconsciousness (throughout our lives we are programmed by society; now is our chance to decide for ourselves what is good for us). In the future you will see that you have fewer and fewer unwanted reactions and more of the alternative reactions that you write down in your diary.

For example: someone spilled coffee on you and you got angry and you let this anger out and yelled at the person, spicing it with choice words. After describing it in your diary, add three alternative ways of reacting: "I let myself yell because I feel above her, I have to pay attention to my ego taking over—don't let the ego take over"; or, "My anger and frustrations have nothing to do with her, she is just the messenger from the universe, I need to be thankful and see why this situation occurred—see the signs and act upon them"; or, "Lately I've been pushing myself and it results in loss of control—I have to work on acting from a present point rather than just following the automatic subconscious behaviors."

The situations you tell your diary can be of any kind or character, not just negative ones. Things where we want to be better or do the right thing. This might include not being brave enough to speak your thoughts, wasting time on the wrong people or situations, not giving as much as you'd like to charity, giving too much or too little support to people around you.

As well as having negative reactions, during an average day we also do some things well, and react in ways we actually like. Write those down too. Give yourself positive enforcement. For example, "That gossiper from work tried to suck me into one of his conversations (trash talks) but I gently refused while my eyes made a clear statement that I don't approve of gossip. He will respect me now he knows I am a person of good principles."

What not to do

Don't make the diary your friend; it is a tool for development, not for sharing or speaking your thoughts and emotions. Write short and sharp.

How and when do I know it's working?

When you find yourself in situations familiar from the past, but your automatic reaction is different. You may even come to find that they match exactly what you have written in your diary.

Why am I doing it?

To change unwanted reactions.

In short

Write, baby, write! Establishing communication with your subconsciousness and reprogramming it gives you another key for control and design of your fate.

Zai mudra

Time and duration

Once, twice a day for around 15–20 minutes.

What to do

Put the hands in *zai mudra* and pass the *mudra* in front of the chakras.

How to do it

Make yourself comfortable, sitting or standing. Open your palms and separate the fingers. Hold them out in front of you with the palms facing away, like you are about to place them flat on a wall ahead of you. Now let the index fingers and the thumbs connect (just move the hands towards each other till they touch). You have a triangle made by the connection of the index fingers and the thumbs (index to index, thumbs to thumbs).

Similarly to the previous exercise about seeing an energetic field, look carefully until you can see something like a screen between the fingers. Put the triangle of fingers and thumbs in front of the point between your eyebrows and look into the energetic screen. Feel the energy flowing within the head. Move the triangle down to the throat chakra. Let the chakra be concentrated on the energetic screen. After a while, you will feel the energetic streams. Keep moving the triangle down to the next chakra and the next one, until you reach the first chakra (don't forget that each chakra has to be concentrated on the screen—not your mind but the chakra). Give each chakra a few minutes. After you have finished, place the triangle around the center of the body (whatever you intuitively think the center is) and concentrate on the screen from the position of the whole body, as though the body is one indivisible unit that is concentrated on the energetic screen.

Thank the *mudra* and the universe.

What not to do

Don't look too long into the triangle with the third eye chakra.

How and when do I know it's working?

You will feel energetic movement in the relevant chakra.

Why am I doing it?

This *mudra* is very mysterious and symbolizes many interesting things. Every spiritual tradition has its own symbols. Some of them have triangles as a symbol. Whatever a certain school attributes to the triangle, this *mudra* can be the embodiment of the attribution. Normally, it symbolizes the upwards movement of energies, or ascension. It connects or helps to attune the energies or vibrations of our bodies with the vibrations of the higher realms, partly by tuning each chakra to the right vibration. The higher energies influence the lower ones, balance and accelerate them, raising the vibrations.

In short

The symbol of the equilateral triangle is the symbol of God or a highest principle. We can connect to this by recreating the triangle with our own hands.

7

Energetic Cleansings

I wish I could have put this section at the start of the book. It is a series of simple (mostly) and effective energetic cleansings.

Those cleansing methods will look absolutely or at least relatively normal to you at this stage, but like the subconsciousness cleansing or the bell exercise, if they had been introduced at the beginning or even in the middle of the book, they would have looked weird and might have driven you away from reading the rest of it. Now that you have reached this stage, you know that all the exercises work.

We have seen that when we come into contact with anyone at any level, we exchange energies. And that it is very important to live using only your own energies. This section will introduce you to enough methods to cleanse all the unwanted energies on every necessary level.

As we have seen throughout the book, energies follow the *will* or the *willpower* and since energetic cleansing includes dealing with energies (we use one kind of energy to remove other kind of energy), we need to have strong will and enough psychic energy.

The cleansings should be performed once a day before bed; it is not recommended to go to sleep without having done them. You can do them at other times too, if or when needed. Some of them we need to perform on rarer occasions, only when they feel necessary. Everything we have discussed regarding the principles of exercises is relevant to these energetic cleansings as well.

There are many theories, methods and rumors around cleansing unwanted energies. After trying many of them, I have found that these are the most reliable. The following set of cleansings is comprehensive (at least up to the stage of development within the remit of this book) and covers all you need as a sensitive person to be free of unwanted energies.

It is vital to go to bed clean, there should be zero other energies in the system. We pass a much deeper stage of alpha waves on our way to the stage of sleeping and the energies we don't want to keep can sink deeper than most of us can reach at this stage, and so would be very difficult to cleanse. We can only cleanse from as deep as we can reach. So if the energy we are about to cleanse is on the surface, let us cleanse it from there.

A simple **contrast shower** can cleanse all the energetic bodies, as well as the physical one. After you finish your regular shower, turn the water to the coldest temperature you can handle. Let it run briefly over the legs, arms and the body. Don't let the water run for very long. Then switch to hot water, the hottest you can handle without burning yourself, and do the same (be careful with the head, which is more sensitive to high temperatures). Then cold again, then back to hot, and finish on cold. The more extreme the temperature is, the better the cleansing will be. You can make the water just a bit colder and hotter every time.

If you do not have access to a shower, just use a sink to wash your hands with cold water, from above the elbows to the fingers.

The contrast shower is, like taking a sauna and then having an ice bath, very good for cleansing, but the level of the cleansing is not sufficient for sensitives. It is good to cleanse the outer body, of course, but we also have a whole reality inside that has to be taken care of. **Yellow rose** cleansing is designed to solve this kind of challenge.

Visualize a yellow rose that has a magnet in it. This magnet's special ability is to attract only foreign energies from your bodies, all the energies that do not belong to you. Place the yellow rose on the top of your head and ask it to attract all the foreign energy from your bodies. The rose will start spinning and getting darker. When it is almost black, gently remove it and take it out of the house to an outside bin (no need to go there physically, just use your will; but you do not want this energy in your house), then put a small bomb in it and let it explode, burning all the energies it has collected from you. Do the yellow rose cleansing as many times as needed to cleanse all the bodies—including the head. Many people forget the head after they have done the bodies.

Don't forget to explode the rose—we don't want this energy to be picked up by others.

When you have finished cleansing with the yellow rose, visualize a **red rose** with a magnet inside. This magnet is able to attract all the energy you have left behind. Place the red rose on the top of the head and ask it to collect all your energies, regardless of where or from when they are (you may well still have residue energy from some time ago, maybe from an occasion when you were angry). As before, the red rose will start spinning, collecting your energies and getting darker the more energy it absorbs. When it is done, connect the red rose with a wire to the center of the Earth and allow all the foreign energies that have been entangled with your energy to go to the center of the Earth, then let the wire explode. Raise the rose a little way above the head and blow it up with a wave of golden energy that will let the energy into the air to form a small cloud around your head. This golden energy is "heavy" and will descend, covering your aura like water, until it reaches the feet and enters the physical body from there. This feels good!

These two rose cleansings must be done every evening before bed and can also be done at any other time, as needed. If you do them while in trance they are even more effective. After you have done the rose cleansings, tell yourself that you forgive everyone, for everything and for good, and that you forgive yourself for everything and for good.

And mean it. When you cannot forgive, you retain some part of the negative energy that connects you with the person you cannot forgive. It is very harmful, first of all to you because you are stuck in the moment, in the past, and you are maintaining the negative connection with your energies. In some sense you cannot go any further in your life because the energy does not flow there.

Some people wake up in the morning (or from an afternoon nap) carrying negative emotions and energies they have brought back from the trip they took while the body was sleeping. You can do the yellow rose exercise once in the morning (or after any other sleep) as well, to cleanse those energies.

If after the roses cleansings you still think there is more to be cleansed, the next exercise answers this challenge. **Inner flame** cleansing is done in a good trance state. Sit, get into trance, place your protections, go to your place, and ask your inner flame to come. It will come in the shape of a candle with a flame. Take the flame, turn into a ball of fire, let it enter from the forehead and pass through your pineal gland and down the spine until it reaches the tailbone and exits the body from there. Do this three times. Then insert the candle with the flame into your head and pass it over everything; let the flame burn every piece of energy that is not yours. Do the same to all the parts of the body. As you move the candle inside the body, some areas may feel like they are blocking the movement of the candle; for example the throat. If this is the case, do not force the candle to pass through the blockage but instead visualize it going outside the body and re-entering it past the blockage. If in some places the feeling is not nice, just do your best to relax this place and let the energy pass through. When you have finished, put the flame back in the candle, leave the candle where you took it from and come back to reality.

Remember the **bell** exercise? This is a very good cleaner. Very often when I cannot find the right place—the inner source or location—and the right cleansing method to use, I just do the bell for a few minutes in every direction. Try it and see how it works for you.

Cobra breathing awakens the inner fire, if you feel that you have caught some energy that you don't like. For example, someone has passed near you and it has left an unpleasant feeling on one side of your body. Concentrate on the place and exhale as in the cobra breathing exercise we did earlier. This will release the energy from your energetic bodies. We can use this method to be cleansed of unwanted energies arising, without being distracted from our meditation.

Normally, meditations begin with calming ourselves and getting into energetic balance. The advantage of this cleansing is that it does not require any specific preparations or prolonged concentration. The slight downside is that it works only on the upper level and cannot cleanse deeper energies.

We have worked hard on our **powers of concentration,** so let us now put them into practice. If you are in a room with someone whose energies you cannot handle, just tell yourself, "I don't want to feel that." Do it with intention, and you will stop feeling that person's energy. Every energy you don't like, you can decide not to feel, or command it not to touch you.

We can combine the **tai chi palms playing** with **concentration.** Use the tai chi palms playing exercise while your concentration is on the plane or spot you are willing to cleanse. We know that where our concentration is, is where the work is done. Another point to be aware of is that negative energy causes lack of energetic flow and this can cause illness. So playing with your palms while concentrating on an energetic channel, a chakra, a spot on the body or the whole stream of the body's energy will move the energy and open the blocks from the place of concentration. The same works for the energetic balls and the bell. Concentrate anywhere that is needed while doing those exercises and see where the energetic work is happening.

Normally when we do the tai chi palms playing we sense weird feelings here and there; those are blockages. You can place your attention on them to cleanse them, but not on the physical body. Remember that we want to work with the subtle bodies because they then influence the physical body.

In a conversation, when you feel that the other person is drinking your energy, you can just decide not to give it to them. In addition, you can move your attention from the person (you can still look and listen but just not pay full attention), cut the energetic connection between you and put a **window** or sheet of glass between you and the other person. It also works for more than one person at a time, and even if your conversation is happening by other means, not face to face.

Sometimes, after we have felt someone's emotions and they have left a deep imprint on us, it can be very hard to get rid of them and we carry the emotions all day. If you visualize a **purple flame** with which you cleanse the navel, solar plexus, heart chakra and the throat, those imprints of foreign emotions will be erased. If it is not effective, you can always first get into trance and then cleanse. But to tell you a secret: if you keep practicing, your subconsciousness will become your consciousness. Maybe you are not at the point of being interested in this at the moment, but spiritual development includes this step. If and when you reach that point, you will be able to do all these valuable things without especially going to trance.

There is an interesting trick for people who live in big cities. We always get to feel everything and everyone, and all of it is so close, no distance.

You can always use the pole of light during the day and change it every now and then. This can be very energy-consuming but it is effective. Another thing is to **ground your aura.** Just visualize that your aura has a wire going to the center of the Earth and grounding you. Every energy that will come into your aura will go to the center of the Earth. One thing is necessary to remember: if you forget about the wire, at some point you will feel pressure from the place you connected with it. If this happens, just move the wire aside, blow it up and visualize a new one. Like with the roses, the more advanced you become, the fewer roses or wires you will need.

There is a universal power that we call **Archangel Michael.** Normally this archetypal energy is depicted as an angel with a sword. We can make use of the energy; or in other words, this energy can help us to cleanse.

There are many creatures we don't know about (and that is good) that stick to us and suck our energies. In many cases they like a specific type of energy. Sometimes we feel like someone is pushing us towards some negative emotional expression, after which we feel exhausted. Remember the film *The Matrix?* We are batteries for creatures that exist outside the matrix (in the astral realm, in our case).

We accumulate many of those creatures during the day and some of them even lay their eggs, so to speak, in our subtle bodies. We can easily cleanse them using the sword of Archangel Michael. We must select one knife and dedicate it only for this purpose.

Note: For safety, please use a blunt knife.

Take the knife, pray to God to help you cleanse and disconnect (I will explain) from everything. Ask the Archangel Michael if you can borrow his sword and visualize your knife in blue flames. Now pass the knife all over the body, starting from the top of the head and moving down. Use downward strokes, like when combing hair. Keep the attention on the blue flame. If needed, pass more than once over areas where you feel it is necessary. (In my case, it is the back side of the heart chakra.) Don't forget the palms and the feet. After you have finished, give the sword back (don't sell it on eBay) and thank God and Archangel Michael. Sounds occult but it is really not; it is a natural force like fire, or the wind. And we use fire and wind, so we can use Archangel Michael's sword.

About the *disconnect* part of the prayer. We make energetic contacts with everyone we come in contact with, whether physically or by thought. In the same manner, people get entangled with us without our awareness. But sometimes people are very angry at us and think of us while they are angry. Remember that we create with our visualization, and that emotions are a very strong booster for the energetic stream. So at the moment of their anger this person created an energetic double of you and put it on the wall (sounds like a voodoo doll, I know). This energetic double is equal to you and their existence lasts as long as yours. By using the angelic sword, we can cut the connections created by other people.

You can also use the sword to cleanse other people (if they agree!), or a room, or our car. If you lack a knife, use your index finger like a knife instead. I'll say again: don't cleanse people without them agreeing; this is black magic and very bad karma. Even if you think that the end justifies the means, it does not. Better to pray for the best outcome possible for the person and send them love. This is all you can do without creating bad outcomes in the future.

As for rooms or any other space, it's fine as long as it is your space and anyone you share this space with agrees to the cleansing. You don't need to be in the room or even the house; you can be in another town, state or hemisphere.

It goes like this: visualize pipes running from up to down in the corners. By corners I mean every place where two walls connect. So in an ordinary square room you will have four pipes in each corner, another four on the floor that create a square and another square on the ceiling. So you have drawn a cube in the room that fits the corners.

Next is a well in the middle of the room that reaches to the center of the Earth. Connect the cube with the well using the same type of pipes. When the construction is ready, say, "All the energy forms in this room, whether thoughts, emotions or any other kind of energy that are harmful and/or don't belong to me, let them burn in the center of the Earth."

As well as at home, you can do it in your office or workplace; but if you have colleagues, ask them if it is okay to cleanse the room. It is good to do it in rooms that don't have a flow of air or that many people come into/use over a day.

───～───

I just want to remind you: don't look at the negative energy you are cleansing from yourself, or it will come back to you.

Afterword

All the information given in the book is to allow you to broaden your knowledge and obtain a better understanding of your sensitivity. When we have learned about balancing it, and about its nature and how to work with it, we can give it the right place and role in our life, which is as a tool for obtaining information through subtle channels. In this way we will see that the sensitivity is not simply a way of life but a highly sophisticated tool that is there to serve us; and with which we can serve others.

Be a good person even if it is hard. Remember that God and the truth are within us; this is why the balance has to come from within and comes from your personal effort and will. Bring light and love to yourself and those around you. You have your own path.

I hope that at this stage a new person is reading those lines. A new person from the point of view of inner balance, who could open the book to its first pages again and feel the difference between yourself back then, and the new you.

Now you will be able to look back and tell how some exercises have influenced you. Energetic balls, bell, morning candle, meditation of eternity all help to bring you into energetic balance, which makes you stronger and less influenced by the energies of others. The pole of light, window and the aura grounding all help to protect.

You are familiar with your subconsciousness and how to communicate with it: you know how to get to your subconsciousness and you know how to perform the minimum required operations for us. You also know that when you awake the energy in an organ, we will see later in the trance state, visions related to this organ's hidden traumas and heavy emotions. This is the subconsciousness communicating with us. And writing a diary as means to communicate with it.

We talk about loving ourselves and loving others. But it is the same love and the same source which is the love of God in our heart. Built-in love. Experience, live and give this love in all the forms you want to. This is what it is all about.

Happiness and satisfaction are achieved when we devote our time to serving others to our best abilities. It is not a coincidence that when we help someone using our talents we experience happiness, joy and satisfaction. The book is mainly about what is important to put a sensitive person into balance; but once you feel safe and calm, some level of happiness will come. Because the job you have done while reading and performing the exercises is the first step towards self-fulfillment. We can fulfill ourselves only when we are in balance and stable. We cannot give much to others while we ourselves are in need.

So, what is next? That depends on your wishes. From the spiritual development point of view, we are here to experience, to create and to serve. While doing so, we learn about the universe and the composition of our own talents and abilities, which is made up of what we have in this incarnation and what we have accumulated in previous incarnations.

We are at the centre of our lives, the headquarter. What we create on the inner level we project outward into manifestation. The more balanced we are, the more our action is connected to the sphere of our happiness the closer we get to fulfilling our destiny.

We have learned about our subtle bodies and a bit about how the subtle bodies interact with reality. But you also have other sets of tools that you have to learn about. Those are your talents and abilities, and learning how, when and how much to use of them is the next step. Think of your sensitivity. I hope you have managed to find a good balance and your quality of life has become a great deal better. But do you know why sensitivity is a tool you possess? Do you know where and when you have to use it? Not you as the everyday you, but you as the soul you were before incarnating on Earth. There are many kinds of brushes, each one right for a particular kind of paint, of line and of surface. You wouldn't paint your house with a tiny brush for thin lines and you wouldn't use a big wall brush to paint on a canvas. This is all clear; but things are less clear when it comes to sensitivity. But because sensitivity is one of the tools in your box, getting to know how to use it, for what purpose, and in combination with what other tools has to be your next step.

To be able to do so, we have to learn about what makes us happy and joyful. There we can find the direction of our life. We came here to do something, something that only we can do. When we were kids, we probably all played the cold and hot game—hiding something in the room and calling out the words "cold" or "hot" depending on how close or far away those who were searching for the object got. It is the same with the universe and us; the closer we get to it, the more energies, joy and happiness we get from it.

After learning what makes us happy, we have to learn about our talents and abilities, the tools we have to master and develop, and how to help others. After learning those tools, we have to make the best mix of our abilities, using our tools in the right ratio, in the right situation, on the right person for the right cause. This is why you came here and you have to learn those lessons.

Of the tools in our box, sensitivity can be the most destructive and difficult to balance, but it is also the one that most boosts your spiritual development.

Be flexible, don't get stuck in your beliefs or principles. If something does not serve your spiritual development or your path, let it go. Free up the space for new energies that will serve and help you.

Forgive more, forgive always and forgive everyone—starting with yourself. I cannot overemphasize the importance of this; if you adopt this principle you will see how much you develop spiritually.

Always ask your heart before doing something, and find the strength to do the right thing. You can get the desired result by good means as well as by bad ones. Believe in the good nature of other people and in their big hearts. There are many good people around you and they will help you. Don't be too proud to receive help. We must maintain the balance of giving and receiving.

Don't lose hope and don't pity yourself. Keep working; moving is moving, no matter how slow. When you get to the desired state don't spend too much time there. Remember that the journey awaits you.

Remember to keep the balance between spending time on your own growth and helping others to grow. There are periods of time when we go inwards, to work and reach our next level, and there are times when we go outwards, to help others. Keep the balance between going inwards and outwards. No one road is ideal, only balance and moving forward. Moving forward, that is, without leaving behind those who are ready to follow our steps and the steps of the great master.

And remember: there is no single thing, exercise, method or remedy that solves all of our issues. With every problem and every energy, the universe is entrusting us with a bigger challenge and bigger opportunity to discover our divine nature. With every challenge the universe will direct us to the right method, knowledge and remedy (just as it brought you to this book). It is the most fabulous and endless journey of a spirit on its path, and the higher we go, the more interesting it becomes . . .

Exercise List

The main exercises are marked in **bold**. The remaining exercises are complementary to the main ones.

Sources

The books listed below are in addition to my one-on-one meetings and group workshop with the self-realized master Dimitar Komitov.

William Walter Atkinson. *Your Mind and How to Use It* (new edition published in 2016 by Andesite Press).

Douglas De Long. *Ancient Healing Techniques: A Course in Psychic and Spiritual Development.* Woodbury, MN: Llewellyn Publications, 2005.

Allan Kardec. *The Spirits' Book.* Self-published, 1857 (new edition independently published in 2018).

Allan Kardec. *The Book on Mediums.* Self-published, 1861 (new edition independently published in 2021).

The Kybalion. Yogi Publication Society, 1908 (new edition independently published in 2020).

Genevieve Lewis Paulson. *Kundalini and the Chakras.* Woodbury, MN: Llewellyn Publications, 2002.

Edwin C. Steinbrecher. *Inner Guide Meditation: A Spiritual Technology for the 21st Century.* Newburyport, MA: Red Wheel/Weiser, 1994.

J. C. Stevens. *Kriya Secrets Revealed: Complete Lessons and Techniques.* Independently published, 2013.

Joshua David Stone. *Soul Psychology: How to Clear Negative Emotions and Spiritualize Your Life.* New York: Wellspring/Ballantine, 2010.

Yogi Ramacharaka. *Hatha Yoga; or, the Yogi Philosophy of Physical Well-being.* 1904 (new edition published 2016 by Wentworth Press).

Yogi Ramacharaka. *Science of Breath.* 1903 (new edition published in 2007 by Book Jungle).

About the Author

Photo by Nevena Rikova

Bertold Keinar studied political science and holds a master's degree in economics and banking. A Reiki healer and student of esoteric and mystic knowledge, he is dedicated to guiding sensitives through the difficulties of daily life and specializes in customizing esoteric techniques to help others. Bertold spent time in Israel and Asia and now lives in Bulgaria.

For more information visit: **www.bertoldkeinar.com**

FINDHORN PRESS

Life-Changing Books

Learn more about us and our books at
www.findhornpress.com

For information on the Findhorn Foundation:
www.findhorn.org